Ditches to Riches

By
Captain Will Smith

Ditches to Riches
By William Smith

© 2019 William Smith

Printed in the United States of America

ISBN 978-1-7329400-9-3

Published by: The Ghost Publishing
Author: Captain Will Smith
Edited by: Eli Gonzalez and Vernon LaVia
Proofread by: Lil Barcaski and Christine James, and Linda Hinkle
Contact info: www.captainwillsmith.com
Cover Design: The Ghost Publishing

Dedication

This book is dedicated to everyone struggling to live a better life.

A better future is not impossible.
I believe in you.
If you believe in yourself,
you can change your world.

Table of Contents

CHAPTER 1 - SINCE WHEN IS IT OKAY TO STRIVE FOR MEDIOCRITY?...**9**

IT STARTS AT HOME 11

NO, YOU DON'T GET A TROPHY... 13

LET ME TELL YOU A LITTLE OF MY STORY 15

CHAPTER 2 - WHO DO YOU SEE?............................. **21**

YOUR PAST IS BEHIND YOU 23

HELP YOURSELF 25

POSITIVITY IS CONTAGIOUS AS IS NEGATIVITY 26

CHAPTER 3 - MINDSET... **29**

EGOTISTIC VS. ALTRUISTIC 31

LIVING IN THE PROBLEM 32

TIME MANAGEMENT.. 34

MR. DUNN.. 37

IT'S NEVER TOO LATE TO DO SOMETHING GREAT 38

CHAPTER 4 - PUT UP OR SHUT UP **41**

EXCUSES 51

CHAPTER 5 - MAKE YOUR BYGONES BE BYGONES **55**

THE LAW OF ATTRACTION 62

USE VS. ABUSE... 62

EMBRACE HUMILITY 64

BE PASSIONATE ABOUT YOUR WORK 65

CHAPTER 6 - SUCCESS IS A STATE OF MIND............... **69**

RANDOM... 69

THE PRISON PIT 72

ROUTINE 75

REFLECTIVE.. 76

GOOD IS THE ENEMY OF GREAT...................................... 79

LOOK WITHIN YOURSELF.. 81

CHAPTER 7 - BREAKING THE CYCLE......................... **85**

CHAPTER 8 - HEALTH IS WEALTH 95

CHAPTER 9 - COMMON SENSE IS NOT SO COMMON 101
   THINK FOR YOURSELF 103

CHAPTER 10 - 7-STEP AWARENESS AND SUCCESS PLAN 109
   7–STEP AWARENESS AND SUCCESS PLAN 109
   I'M HERE TO HELP 117

ABOUT THE AUTHOR 121

ACKNOWLEDGMENTS 123

Chapter 1

Since When Is It Okay to Strive for Mediocrity?

Our forefathers would hang their heads in shame if they talked to a teenager today. They came from all walks of life, from different parts of the world, spoke different languages, most had no money to speak of, and yet they carved out a life for themselves in a world filled with danger, lawlessness, and hardship. The next generation took on the challenge and continued to build this country, with blood, sweat and tears. I'm not writing that because it's poetic or cliché, they literally spilled blood, sweated on their fields, farms, or wherever they worked, and buried their loved ones along the way.

Generation after generation of hard-working people flocked to a place where they could live free of tyranny and make a life. In just a couple hundred years, they built the most powerful and economically stable country on the planet. Then came World War II and the Great Depression, and the children of those generations stepped up and elevated this country to heights not equaled yet in modern history. Tom Brokaw, a famous television journalist, best known for being the anchor and managing editor of *NBC Nightly News* for 22 years, then wrote his book, *The*

Greatest Generation, and branded that generation as the best ever. These men went to fight against evil and the women traded their aprons for full-time jobs and kept the economy moving. They were awesome.

Up until that point, generation after generation, we just kept getting better and better. We built factories, produced products never seen before at unheard of quantities, and we even

We built factories, produced products never seen before at quantities unheard of, and even established and mastered the art of flight.

mastered the art of flight. We built the tallest buildings in the world and cities popped up all over our borders. We were on a roll.

But, have you talked to a teenager today? What happened to the work ethic this country was founded upon? The apple has fallen a long, long way from the tree.

Most of the young people today, and I know I might come off sounding like a bitter old grandfather rocking in his porch-chair wearing suspenders and sipping on iced tea, but what I'm going to say is true – most of the young people today feel they are entitled to many of the things that generations before them had to work very hard for. If we as a society don't recognize our folly, we as a country are going to be in big trouble in a generation or two. That's the bad news. The good news? We can fix our own mistakes.

It starts at home

One of the biggest reasons why our children are the way they are, and by children I'm referring more to kids from 12 years old to 25, is because of the erosion of the family unit. Things used to be much simpler with just dad, mom, brother(s), sister(s), and maybe Fido. That nucleus, that safe haven for love, laughter, ideas, growing pains, teaching, lectures, television time spent together, has faded from most of the modern day families.

The American Psychological Association (APA) says that 90% of people marry by the age of 50. Unfortunately, 40-50% of first marriages end in divorce. And, for people who are married more than once, the divorce rate is closer to 70%. The APA goes on to say that children raised in a home where their parents are married are better protected from mental, physical, educational, and social problems.

The truth is, it's not easy staying married and that's not the fault of our children. In most homes, both parents have to work. As a result, we've traded parenting time for money-making time, and it's hurt all of us big time. The responsibility, or much of it, then falls to our educational system to not only instruct and teach our children but also to guide and parent them. It's a mess.

Many Millennial's today grew up in separated families. We live in a world where millions of children don't have a male father figure in the house. The children get to go to Dad's on some weekends, that is, those children whose father's want to be a part of their lives. Those fathers, happy to spend time with their children, hold off on correcting their kids as effectively as they would if they were living with them, more focused on becoming buddies than fathers.

Other fathers, bitter for their own reasons, decide that paying child support is sufficient enough and they choose not to physically or emotionally be with their kids. After all, many women and much of society have told them that what their children really need is their money. So, they buy their way out of accepting responsibility and raising respectful young men and women. On the other end, mothers are trying to fill both roles, so while they still try to be nurturers , they also try to be fathers, which at best, is to imitate a father through the lens of a mother.

No Child Left Behind, told our children who it was okay to fail.

Society tried to step in to help give confidence to every child and made it even worse. One initiative, No Child Left Behind, told our children who it was okay to fail. It reprimanded parents for setting standards or demanding a high level of expectation. It became okay to come in last place. It was a total mess.

This country, built by courage, tenacity, teamwork, and hard work, had created a culture around striving to reach our goals and winning … now tells children it's okay to fail. In youth sports, winning teams aren't the only ones who get trophies, losers get trophies too.

No, you don't get a trophy

I'm sorry that I'm not sorry if this offends people but no one should get an award for last place. Not everybody deserves a trophy. I'm a believer that if you don't work to earn something, you shouldn't cry and throw a tantrum if you don't get it.

Have you heard of Stephanie Krueger? She had worked hard, trained four days a week in dance and gymnastics for the last 10 years. Her goal? To make the prestigious Black Squad – Hanover Park High School's top tier cheering team. The elite team was judged on, among other things, jumps, grace, and choreography.

So, she trained.

For years.

Since she was a child.

As a sophomore, her hard work – getting up early to go to practice and workouts, eating healthier than she wanted to, constantly flipping, sometimes falling, and getting back up and having the courage to be flipped again – paid off. She made the team! Stephanie Krueger was now a member of the elite Black Squad. She was elated. Her parents were elated. And the other girls who made the team and their families were also elated. However, one mother wasn't happy. Not at all.

Her daughter cheered at a higher grade level but didn't make the Black Squad. So, she complained.

Inexplicably, to me anyway, the school decided the squads needed to be more inclusive and allow every cheerleader in the 11th and 12th grades to make the team. And, just like that, due to the complaint of one parent, all of Stephanie's hard work and dedication to her craft became a big waste of time.

Even sadder than what they did to Stephanie and the other young women who deserved to make that elite team, is what they taught these young women they allowed onto the team, even though they didn't work as hard for it and become good enough to earn it. The problem is, real life is not like that. You won't pitch for the Yankees just because you like baseball. You won't play quarterback for the Dallas Cowboys because you play touch football games with your friends on Thanksgiving break. You have to strive to be the best to get to the top.

Evidently, some would read this and find nothing wrong with what happened to Stephanie and the girls that originally made the Black Squad. That's the world we live in. But for those of us who do, guess what … we can rise to the top easier than ever before. If you've got the inner drive and the mental fortitude to be successful, you can. Although there's more competition than ever before, the competitors are watered down versions of what they should be. You don't have to be that way.

Let me tell you a little of my story

I was a "hot shot" young pilot, as some called me for U.S. Airways. At the age of twenty-five, I was flying planes, making great money, and had great friends. I was pretty much living my dream. Then, I was wrongfully convicted and sentenced to federal prison, a conviction that would later be overturned. However, before it was, I spent twenty-six hellish months in jail.

While in prison, being subjected to cruelty and evil I had never experienced, most of my supposedly "good" friends and close family members disowned me. While I was being recruited by gangs, literally fighting to eat my lunch, and being judged by my race and not my character, my dream life turned into a nightmare. Day after miserable day, knowing I was innocent, was a challenge. Each day I fought despair, hopelessness, and went to sleep grumbling about the injustice of it all.

Being that I had accumulated a certain amount of wealth, I was able to hire top legal talent to represent me. We fought vigorously against the corruption that had derailed my life day.

After a too lengthy a stay in a prison, I was exonerated and told I could rejoin society and resume my life. Those were the sweetest words I had ever heard. However, on "the outside", as we prisoners referred to it, everything had changed for me. I made the tough decision to leave the place where I had grown up, a place I loved, and so I moved to Florida to start over.

One of my few remaining friends allowed me to crash on his couch. He was also kind enough to help me get a job. No, it wasn't flying planes … it was digging ditches. When I was taking a break from digging ditches, I was carrying boulders. That's what you do when you're the low man on the totem pole for a landscaping company. I, who used to fly over the clouds, had to keep my head down and pound the earth for its minerals. I helped dig holes for ponds, deck foundations, new homes, and many other things that needed a good digging.

It was backbreaking work. Not to mention the fact that there was no respite from the Florida sun, which is different than the sun many other people across the country know. I did that work, day after day, six or seven days a week, for a whopping $6 an hour.

I could have easily given up. I wanted to many times. My prior life had been unjustly stolen from me. Nothing was fair. I

I should not have had to dig ditches in the Florida heat for $6 an hour! Yet, I did.

should not have had to dig ditches in the Florida heat for $6 an hour! Yet, I did. I knew I had to dig myself out of the hole I was in and unfortunately for me, I had to do this by literally digging holes.

I was able to purchase an old '86 Camino, and I smile as I write this because it was ghastly. But, against all evidence pointing to the contrary, it never let me down. I made it, barely, to and from work each and every day. As I would drive there, dig, carry boulders, and drive back, I set some goals and got to work on reaching them. I didn't stop to think that the goals I had set were too lofty or ridiculous for a guy in my situation. I was too busy getting busy reaching them.

For the first year, I did not date. I did not go to bars. I did not spend the little money I made frivolously. My focus was on my two sons and getting back in their lives. A year later, I had saved up enough money to get an apartment. 365 days is more than plenty of time to sleep on a couch. My kids finally had a place to visit me. Life was getting better.

I applied for a Pell Grant six months later and went back to college. I got a two-year degree in Architectural Design and Construction Technology. Fortuitously for me, the housing boom had started, so I got my CAD certification. I applied and got accepted to a local architectural firm and met Larry Brindley, who would become a lifelong friend. If you read my first book, you'll recognize Larry as my advocate when I was unjustly imprisoned. We worked great together, he as the lead architect and me as one of the project managers.

My life was back on track. I had a good paying job, friends again, and was an active parent in the lives of my sons. Then, while I was in the midst of purchasing a home, the housing bust came. There was a layoff at the architectural firm, and I was let go. It was a tremendous blow for me. I could have taken money from the government, collected welfare, except that ... well, that's just not how I'm built.

A friend offered me a job in pest control. Not the most glamorous job to be sure, but it was a job. I worked all over the Tampa Bay area as a pest control technician. When depression or disappointment tried to bring me down, I thought two things:

1. I *get* to go to work today. (That's a different mindset from those who say I *have* to go work today.)
2. I'm so grateful I'm not digging ditches.

My new career was not producing enough income so I asked the boss if there was anything else I could do to help the company (and myself).

"When you're killing bugs for people, see if you can upgrade the level of service we provide them," he told me.

The next day, my career as a salesperson began. They offered me 20% of what I sold and in the first year, I nearly made six figures. In an effort to sell our services better I studied pesticides, how they work, how they kill, and how they're made. It changed my entire perspective on the industry. *Pesticides are bad for you, folks!*

Two years later, I started Pest Hammer, my own organic alternative to pest control. Right about that time, I borrowed five-thousand dollars from a neighbor and purchased my home. My sons and my mother came to live with me. While that was as wonderful as it sounds, Pest Hammer was just starting out and I had given all I had to buy my house. In other words, I was house-broke. (That's the term homeowner's use when they have absolutely no money but want to remind people who at least they have a house).

I had set goals and was starting to fall away from achieving them. I did the only thing that seemed logical to me. I got another full-time job. If you're a business owner, you know how ridiculous that sounds, to have another full-time job while trying to make your own business profitable. As nonsensical as it sounded, it was the only thing I could do to keep my family together and reach my goals.

I was working more than 80 hours a week on my business and my other job. I didn't take any vacation. I didn't take weekends off. I didn't splurge on extravagant dinners, clothes, or cars. I worked at Pest Hammer and when I wasn't working there, I worked as a laborer for a lawn company. The one constant positive that came from all of that was that sleep came very easy to me every night.

Four years later, I had built up Pest Hammer and sold it for a quarter of a million dollars. The payoff was tremendous. The people who knew about it congratulated me but they had no idea how much I worked for it. It took all the determination and inner drive I could possibly muster.

Shortly before I sold my company, I met a man who would open the way for me to change my life. His name is Matt Fonk. He had a property management company and had hired Pest Hammer for their organic pest control needs. (Sorry, I can't get the sales jargon out of my head).

"I see you have the word 'pilot' in your email. Are you a pilot?" he asked.

I hadn't flown in years, but I never thought of myself as not a pilot, ever.

"Yes, I am."

That conversation was the genesis of getting me back to the skies. My life was literally about to take off into new dimensions. But, only because I worked my tail off to get where I was so that Matt could ask me if I was a pilot.

My question for you is this: What do you want to get out of your life?

My follow-up question, because every good salesperson should have a follow-up question: How hard are you willing to work for it?

Chapter 2

Who Do You See?

When you look in the mirror, who do you see? I'm not asking about what you're wearing or how you hair is done. I'm not asking about the dressed up, dolled up version of yourself because anyone can change their clothes in just a few minutes. Nor am I asking about how good looking or not good looking you are or how fit or overweight you might be. I'm not asking what you see. What you see is the exterior visage that encompasses the person underneath. I'm asking you, when you look in the mirror, who do you see.

Do you know you? The real you? Do you like you?

It's not a rhetorical question. At all. This could be the most serious question anyone has ever asked you. After all, only you really know who you are. You know if you're a good, trustworthy person who works hard for what you want or if you're word doesn't mean much or if you try to skate through life hoping to land on your feet.

Who are you? Do you like you?

Living a successful life starts and ends with being happy with who we see in the mirror. Let's forget about fancy cars, big houses, cool boats, private jets, and drinking the best bubbly for a moment, none of that would matter if you didn't like who you are anyway in terms of being happy with yourself. Do you like who you see staring back at you, knowing your biggest wins, biggest failures, deepest regrets, and those things no one might ever know about you?

Most people will answer the question of if they like themselves by basing it on where they are at the moment. If you don't like yourself because of where you are, here's a cold, hard reality slap for you that I hope you can take – *your best thinking and decision making got you where you are today.*

If you are in debt, you got yourself there.

If you're working at a job you feel is beneath you, you got yourself there. If you're in a relationship you hate, you got yourself there. If you are in debt, you got yourself there. If you haven't had a job in a while, you got yourself there. If you love your life, you got yourself there too!

However, whether or not you like yourself should not be predicated by the present moment. Moments change, surroundings change, relationships change, financial situations change, yet you are the only true constant in your life.

Your past is behind you

Life happens. So does death. So does bad luck. So do tragedies. So do betrayals and many other bad things. Unfortunately, millions of people are still being negatively affected by something that has happened to them and it has hindered their ability to reach their future potential. They carry the guilt, shame, or burden of a loss like an anchor that holds them in place in the river of life.

I lost my father when I was 28. My sister was 46. I was going through the worst time of my life, a time I don't wish on anyone. I had been falsely accused and convicted of a crime and forced to do time in prison. It was there, while I fought despair every moment of every day, when I heard of my father's passing. The fact that I could not be there and grieve with my family and be there to lay him to rest was nearly more than I could bear. However, inexplicably, the sun rose the following morning and I had to deal with the hellish conditions I was living in. My sister, who had all the freedom in the world, didn't handle it as well.

She was already reeling from a divorce, her second one, and losing our dad gave her every bit of justification she needed to literally throw in the towel and give up on her life. She started drinking much more than she normally did. She upped the ante and also started to mix her vodka drinks with drugs, either from the street or from over the counter. One night, nearly a year after our father's death, she passed out from mixing vodka and morphine and never woke up. The two depressants slowed her heart rate down to the point that it stopped beating. She died in her sleep.

During the last years of her life, she would spend the time complaining. She never stopped. She always had a reason for her displeasure. If it wasn't the first husband that gave her the right to be upset, it was the second. If it wasn't the second husband, it was her job situation. If it wasn't her job situation, it was one of her children. Regardless of the situation, during the last years of her life, she felt that she was entitled to complain. She would say she complained a lot because she was miserable when the truth was, she was miserable because she complained a lot.

We all walk through periods of valleys. Some are deeper and darker than others, for sure, but we all go through them. While I was unjustly imprisoned – and yes, I'm going to mention that from time to time, not as a complaint, but to remind you of how far down my own valley went – not only did my father pass away, but my brother-in-law did as well, and we were close. A very dear family friend also passed away as well as my grandmother. I told you, it was a hellish twenty-six months I spent in prison and not all of it was because of what happened inside the prison walls.

I learned, and I want to make sure I impart this to you, not to hang onto the past. When I got out, I couldn't curl up in a fetal position and spend my days crying about injustice or the loss of people who I truly loved. I would have liked to. I thought I even had the right to and that no one would give me grief over it. But, I couldn't. I had a life to restore –

MINE! So I learned that when you hold onto your past, you don't have anything to grab a hold of your future.

Whatever justification you have to be miserable, let it go. Whatever justification you have to be depressed, let it go. Whatever justifies you not to move forward in your life, give yourself the permission to release it. You can read as many self-help books as there are but the only way you can help yourself is by giving yourself permission to move on.

Help yourself

There are millions of good-hearted people out there who *try* to help others but you can't truly help someone until you've helped yourself. Until you've forgiven yourself. Until you've moved on from under the valley that has cast a shadow over your future.

Before a flight, an attendant stands before you and one of the things he or she says is this...

"In the event of a decompression, an oxygen mask will automatically drop in front of you. To start the flow of oxygen, pull the mask toward you. Place it firmly over your nose and mouth, secure the elastic band behind your head, and breathe normally."

He or she continues to say,

"Although the bag does not inflate, oxygen is flowing to the mask. If you are traveling with a child or someone who requires assistance, secure your mask on first, and then assist the other person."

Basically, what they tell you is, during an emergency, as much as you'd like to play the hero, make sure you secure your own safety before trying to save others, otherwise you're going to pass out and not be of use to anyone, including yourself. I'm not sure if it's sad, ironic, or funny but our society is full of people giving advice to others about something they know absolutely nothing about. You can't help someone if you can't help yourself!

I heard somebody with no job, collecting money from the government to feed him and his family, start a sentence to someone else like this, "Let me show you how to make money …" Sadly, that's not the worst of it. The worst part is that the other person, knowing the guy about to "drop knowledge" can't support himself or his family, is actually listening for nuggets of wisdom that will assuredly catapult his or her finances!

The truth is, getting yourself out of whatever predicament you're in, starts and ends with you.

Positivity is contagious as is negativity

Some children love baseball. They love to watch it on TV or in person. They start to play it and love to play it. They like it so much, they get baseball cards, hoping to get some of their favorite players. They ask their parents for jerseys of their favorite players. They practice it, wanting to get good at it. They gravitate to other kids who love to play baseball. When they all get to high school, they all make the team. Their individual passion brings them together and collectively, they push one another to be the best players they can be.

It's important to surround yourself with people with similar interests and goals. It's one of the laws of attraction. In 2006, Rhonda Byrne wrote a best-selling book called *The Secret*. The book was based on the film with the same name earlier in the year. The book and movie reintroduces the notion originally popularized by people such as Madame Blavatsky and Norman Vincent Peale, which suggest that focusing your mental energies and thinking about certain things will make them appear in one's life.

The message in the book and the film highlight the importance of gratitude and visualization in achieving one's desires, along with alleged examples. Basically, her point is that if you think on something long and hard enough, somehow, someway, you're going to be able to achieve it. She doesn't call upon a specific higher power but instead says "the universe" will bring that thing you constantly think about.

I don't speak to the validity of what "the universe" can or cannot do, but I do believe in the core premise of her teaching. If you spend your time thinking of doom and gloom, that nothing will ever go right, and that you can never succeed – then you'll be right, you'll never succeed. Conversely, if you spend your time thinking positively, speaking words of encouragement and life, and believing that you are going to be a success, as long as you put in the work that coincides with those thoughts, you'll be successful.

Your success starts in your mindset before it materializes. The battle is between your ears.

The battle is between your ears.

Sometimes, you can't go by what you see. For more than a year, I saw a sofa as my bed. Sometimes, you can't go by what you hear. I heard I was a convicted felon that would never fly again. Your mind has to be a safe haven for your goals, dreams, and aspirations.

Embrace positive thinking. Allow yourself to believe that you deserve to be successful. You do. You deserve to be successful. You deserve to own that luxury car. You deserve a second chance and you deserve to crush it the second time around. But it makes no difference if I believe that for you but you don't. You need to believe it.

If you can change your thinking, if you can change the way you think about yourself, your journey, and your destination, you'll change your life. That's not a secret.

Chapter 3

Mindset

"Success is to be measured not so much by the position that one has reached in life as by the obstacle which he has overcome while trying to succeed."
Booker T. Washington, Author
Up from Slavery: An Autobiography

What does success mean to you? Can you envision it? At this point, you're most likely thinking of a big house with many rooms, elegant chandeliers in the foyer, plush carpet, priceless pieces of art on stands or lit perfectly on walls. As your focus zooms out, you probably see a pristine swimming pool with a few high-priced luxury cars encompassed by lush, vivid green, freshly mown grass and a long winding driveway that leads to a gate adorned by a family crest.

Is that it? Is that all success means? Money?

What if I told you that success shouldn't be measured by what you have but by how many people you've helped? People have asked me, "Will, what does it take to be successful?" and I know they're looking for a silver bullet idea on how they can become rich. *The truth of it is this, success and money do go hand in hand. But the best way to become successful financially is to help others. The more people you help, the more successful you will become.* If you're in a sales job and wake up every morning thinking how many people you can sell that day, you're going to continuously be outsold by your competitor that thinks, "How many people can I help today?"

When you do a deep dive though and really contemplate what success means, is it really money? Brilliant actor/comedian Robin Williams was, what most people would consider, successful. Famous designer Kate Spade, who had her line of purses sold in millions of stores around the world was, what most people would consider, successful. But, were they really? Then why did they commit suicide?

The truth of it is that money, wealth, power, and fame does not equate to happiness. Some of the richest kings in history were paranoid and schizophrenic. They could have anything they wanted, anyone they wanted. They were the complete authority and were not subject to anyone or anything. Yet, we wouldn't trade our lives for theirs once we knew the amount of pressure that was on them.

Success is a tricky word to define, my friends. I believe that of all the religions, Buddhism has come to define success best. Their happiness, their joy, their zeal for life doesn't come from material possessions. It comes from an inner peace that drives them to help others.

Egotistic vs. altruistic

Egotistical people strive for what they want. They want it so badly, they think that what they want, they actually need. They will go through however many people they have to, and they'll lie, cheat, and double-cross anyone who gets in the way of their success.

To a degree, we're all egotistical though, aren't we? We all take a little more than we need. Don't think so? Go to a buffet. Tell me that you don't put more food on your plate than you know you'll ever eat? It's natural to want to be secure financially, to have more. But, success stops being success when it comes at the price of your inner being, your soul.

Altruistic people are defined as people who are characterized by acts that don't benefit them personally but that are beneficial to other individuals. They're the ones who we tend to gravitate to when times are bad. The ones who give sound advice. The ones who don't just say they'll help you move but will actually show up with coffee for everyone before the moving van gets there.

The answer I tell people when they ask me, "How can I be successful?" is ... "Be altruistic." It's simple, really. When you're selfless, you don't diminish, you grow. You become content based on your actions that help others. Karma is a funny thing. Oftentimes it will repay acts of kindness with strong, true friendships and a sense of community and belonging, which are the foundations for a life well lived.

Living in the problem

People who live in the problem, die in them. Generally, the problems are self-inflicted. Self-absorbed people will blame everyone but themselves, even though they got themselves in their predicament. However, that's not even the worst part. The worst part is they spend more time complaining – falsely accusing others for their situation – than on finding the solution. Because they think their problems come from the acts of others, they expect the solution to come from others.

>...they spend more time complaining – falsely accusing others for their situation – than on finding the solution.

The best way to get out of a problem is by establishing a strong foundation. Reggae artist, EEK-A-MOUSE says it best in the opening lyrics to his song, *Noah's Ark:*

>*The wise man builds his house on the rock*
>*The foolish man builds his house on the sand*
>*And when the rain came tumbling down*
>*The foolish man house it washed away*

At this point in time, you may or may not feel that you have a strong foundation. That's okay. You have time to build it. It starts with an unwavering commitment to better your life. Where you are at this moment does not have a bearing on where you decide to get to in life. If you're sleeping at a friend's house, with no job, with a bad past, with no idea of what you're going to do with your life, that's okay. That's where I started. *You just have to decide to not dwell on your situation and act on getting out of it. You need a short-term plan and a long-term plan.* Your short-term plan should center on getting a job, and your long-term plan, if your desire is to be wealthy, should center on owning a business. In life, the winners play the long game. It starts with education.

Educating yourself is paramount to a strong foundation. You can throw a rock and hit 15 idiots, they're all over the place. People with wisdom and knowledge can carve out their own destinies. Build your foundation by getting a job and then get to a night school.

Sadly, our education system is horrible. They make every allowance for failure. For example, Billy can study hard, discipline himself, and get great grades and graduate while at the same time, Sammy can be disruptive, not do his homework and fail … only to go to summer school for a week or two and graduate with the same degree Billy has earned. However, once they get to the real world, Sammy is in for a rude awakening.

Sammy might get the same degree as Billy but the Sammy's of the world will end up working for the Billy's of the world. Sammy's hard work, his sweat, time, energy, and talent will go towards making Billy's dreams a reality. *One of the things to build your foundation on is this knowledge – you are not entitled to a great life. You must work for it.*

Your current situation might be your current reality but it doesn't have to be your future. Stop complaining about this and that and take ownership of your life. Assume the responsibility that your life is dependent on your choices and actions or inactions.

Time Management

"We are what we repeatedly do.
Excellence, therefore, is not an act but a habit."
Aristotle

Is it me or does it seem that everyone has a severe case of Attention Deficit Hyperactivity Disorder (ADHD)? In the medical world, mainly children and teens suffer from being so hyperactive that they are unable to control their impulses. It's considered the most commonly diagnosed form of mental illness. To a degree, I believe that this sickness has gone from affecting children and now affects adults.

The largest group of people who are joining social media sites today are women over the age of 55. It seems that even our grandmothers have a good old-fashioned case of ADHD. In years past, grandma was counted on to watch the grandkids while the parents went out on a night on the town. Now, most of the grandmas seem to be out on the town, far too busy to help nurture little Suzie.

It may seem like I'm digressing but I'm laying a foundation to make a point. One of the biggest obstacles you will face when trying to better your life are distractions. They come in many forms. Now, more than ever, it's important to maximize the power and clarity that comes from knowing how to manage your time wisely.

Too many people are busy trying to do too many things. In fact, they try to do so many things that very few things ever get done. Many people start many projects, they just don't get finished. I've developed a little system that works out great for me. I'll share it with you in the hopes that you can draw from it.

I'm usually at my computer Monday – Friday by 7 a.m. I give myself two hours to answer emails, do a little surfing, read about the weather and other things of interest to me as a pilot or a person. After 9 a.m., I don't check my emails. If there's ever some sort of emergency, the people who would have to get me know my cell phone number. From 9 till about noon, I'm either taking the kids to school or in business meetings. If I'm flying that day, I'm usually taking off around noon and returning around 5 p.m.

Naturally, not every day is the same but as long as I'm in control, that's typically my day. The biggest challenge for me, and I think to most people, is eliminating distractions. The invention of the cellular phone may go down as one of the best inventions in the history of mankind. We literally have the information of most of the known world in the palm of our hands. Through Google and other search engines, we can find out most of our answers in 15 seconds. Through services like Netflix and Hulu, we can watch movies of every genre and choose from perhaps hundreds of quality television shows. Through social media sites such as Facebook, Instagram, or LinkedIn, we can catch up on all of our friends, family, and acquaintances. Cell phones are a necessary component to

We literally have the information of most of the known world in the palm of our hands.

our lives. However, with all of their benefits come myriad distractions. Some distractions by cell phones have been deadly. In fact, texting while driving is as dangerous as drinking alcohol and driving.

Those incessant beeps and blips that notify us when someone has mentioned us, when an email has entered our inbox, when a friend likes or comments on a post — they're incredibly distracting. I suggest that when you're doing whatever it is you do to make a living, just do that. Turn off the notifications on your social media apps and on other things that aren't absolutely necessary.

If dad gets home at 6, family time should start at 6:30 with the cell phones off so you can share the experiences of the day you've just lived. Enjoy family time; it's not infinite. If you have children now, remember they won't always live with you. Turn your cell phone off at 9 p.m., read a book, work on the thing you love to do so that you don't have to make a living doing something you'd rather not do.

Another big time waster is when time is spent with the wrong people. You don't see Warren Buffet hanging out with potheads who aren't goal oriented. Remember, if you lie down with dogs, you'll get up with fleas. If you want to be a plumber, start hanging out with plumbers. If you want to be a truck driver, hang out with truck drivers. Get into their world. I became a pilot again by once again spending time at airports and airplane hangers. You don't see the dregs of life chartering or flying million-dollar jets.

Mr. Dunn

There is nothing you've gone through that you cannot recover from. I'm living proof but I'm not the only one. Success stories abound in every city and town across this country and the world. There are some people who have been handed a horrible deck of cards who didn't make excuses for why they couldn't get out, they just worked on getting out. Warrick Dunn is one of those people.

Warrick was born in New Orleans, LA on January 5, 1975. Dunn's mother, Betty Smothers, was a police officer. Periodically, she would pick up extra shifts when they were available, leaving Warrick to watch over his younger siblings. Betty had a goal to realize the American Dream of home ownership. However, in 1993, while working an extra shift, she was shot and killed in a robbery attempt. It was now up to Warrick to raise his younger siblings full time.

One of the big problems in terms of time was that Warrick was an incredibly talented football player. Despite the many challenges, Warrick had a great career at Florida University, the Tampa Bay Buccaneers and Atlanta Falcons.

As impressive as his football career was, the reason why I'm mentioning him now is because of his philanthropy.

Today, Warrick Dunn Charities, Inc. is a non-profit organization that improves the lives of many people through innovative programming inspired by his life journey. He has received local and national recognition for his philanthropic work including winning the Walter Payton Man of the Year Award in 2005, the 2010 Heisman Humanitarian Award, and the 2011 Jefferson Humanitarian Award for Public Service, along with many others.

Warrick Dunn was an incredible athlete. He is one of the 31 men to rush for more than 10,000 yards in NFL history (he is 22nd all-time, right behind O.J. Simpson at 21). I appreciate his athleticism, toughness, and grit but it fails in comparison to how much I appreciate his heart to help others. As of this writing, he still partners with Habitat for Humanity to build homes for disadvantaged families across the U.S. To date, they have partnered to build more than 155 homes for single moms and their kids. Most of the homes come fully furnished, "all the way down to the toothbrushes in the bathroom," he said in a *Sports Illustrated* article.

It's never too late to do something great

After living a great life as a pilot for a major airline, I was 32 years old with no money, a felony record, and no prospects. I've already shared part of my story but I'll reiterate some of it here, hopefully to drive another important point into your thought process. I worked two full-time jobs while going to college. Please read that sentence again and allow it to sink in.

I had to be selfish with my time. I knew if I spent my time hanging around or looking for dates, it would lengthen the time it would take for me to reach my goals. Wherever you are in life, whoever you are, whatever you've done, I want to encourage you not to give up. Think big. If I hit the restart button at 32, if you're 25 or 45, you can too.

It doesn't matter if you have a rap sheet. I'm living proof, as are many more who have gone to jail and got out to live great lives and do big things. Why not you? Search inside yourself and find your inner drive. You have it. We all have it. Like muscles, you just might have to exercise it before you can see the gains. How you handle the tough situations will determine your success.

Dig deep. You can master discipline, sacrifice, and consistency. You know you can. It doesn't matter if you've never been able to up to this point in your life. You can start fresh. Success starts with the right mindset.

Chapter 4

Put Up or Shut Up

The time for action started for me when I was digging ditches. I understood that while working for someone else is okay, it could also be a trap if I developed that into a routine. I didn't want to be a worker, I wanted to be business owner. I wanted full control over my life and my finances. I put pride aside and asked my neighbor for some help. He took a chance on me and loaned me five-thousand dollars. I used the money to buy a truck and a trailer with the intention to do pest control. Before then, I had been working in sales and upselling for a termite repair company – getting leads from other termite inspectors where there were damaged homes. Using my skills as a framer, I could find the termites and make repairs as needed. I started with what I had, which, with the loan and the new equipment, allowed me to go full-tilt into starting the pest control company.

Launching my own business in an already crowded marketplace while still being relatively new to the area was daunting. My work ethic was my saving grace; I was willing to work 12 hours a day, 6 days a week. Watching me work at full capacity made my neighbor feel good about loaning me the money. My collateral was my work ethic, and he knew he would be paid back in-full and then some. It was important for me to have him know I was a good, safe bet.

Once I got underway, I kicked it into overdrive and grew the business. As a business owner, you wear many hats. During the day, I would spray houses, and make afternoon calls. At night, I would do all my invoicing and accounting. I figured out a way to build my own website, got an account with QuickBooks, and ran my business through my iPhone.

I put away enough money to live on and always made sure I paid my phone bill on time as that was my lifeline to work. I did my grocery shopping on Fridays and stuck to a tight budget. I wouldn't buy more than I needed and learned to save on my electric bill. I would cut down on electricity when I wasn't in the house by shutting off the breaker box. Every little thing that is plugged in uses power. I didn't need those things to be running while I wasn't there so by shutting things down, I also kept my bill down. I put a timer on my water heater to only heat it when I needed. I cut corners in every way I could and got only the things I needed, not the things I thought I wanted.

No one *needs* a Starbucks coffee, energy drinks, or cigarettes. Those are wants and should not be confused with necessities. It's one thing to treat yourself or indulge now and again but not every day if you're trying to get to another plateau. In my case, I was driven to success and did all the little things I could to make sure I would reach my goal. I saved and saved and then saved some more. I even started a small IRA for my retirement. Do you want to work till 85 or retire at 60? I knew the answer to that question and started working toward it day by day.

Another thing I did that was both fiscally and emotionally sound was to STOP trying to date. It wasn't as easy as it sounded. You first have to be emotionally involved with yourself before you can be in any way involved with anyone else. If you're broken, you're going to break someone else if you attempt to be in a loving relationship with him or her. Be steadfast and disciplined. Rebuild yourself; love yourself first or you will crumble at the first deterrent. Like who you are or change whatever it is about yourself you don't like so you can like you.

Be steadfast and disciplined.

Getting into a relationship with someone battling something like drugs or alcohol is a bad idea. NA and AA advocate no dating because you will fail. If this is you, consider what I'm saying. For me, I needed to get back to a place where I was stable, emotionally and financially, before I got involved with anyone.

I needed to focus on success and my sons. That was enough for me to handle considering the traumatic experience I had been through. When you depend on other people for love, everything becomes about that person. You eat, live, and breathe for them. If the relationship deteriorates, you deteriorate. Depression sets in. You lose focus and start a decline that can lead to failure in other parts of your life. I could not let that happen to me after all I had been through, so for those years, I stayed single and it made all the difference in my climb back up. By the way, my goal wasn't to get to the top, it was to get to the sky!

Due to honest, hard work and earning happy customers that were willing to give me referrals, my business took off. Before I knew it, I was able to hire some new people. I brought on two more technicians to actually run the routes, which allowed me to focus on marketing and managing the business. I started attending social networking events, which led to a whole world of marketing opportunities, and eventually, a whole lot more.

A lucky happenstance occurred due to one simple ad. I was advertising my business on Craigslist because it was free and I needed all the business I could get. A man named Matt Fonk answered my ad. He managed a number of properties, all of which needed pest control. We began communicating via email, and he saw the word pilot in my email address. "Say, Will, are you actually a pilot?" he asked at one point and I told him I had been and hoped to return to it as soon as possible. It turned out he was a member of a flying club, and he invited me to attend one of their meetings on Davis Island with the concept that I might join the club. There I met other like-minded pilots.

One of them wanted to start a charter company, and I told him about my experiences as a pilot. He wanted me to be an instructor for him. I told him I didn't have a whole lot of money to rent airplanes, so he said he would lend me a plane and help me renew my certification as a flight instructor. A pilot's license doesn't expire so I was good there, and I was able to get the FAA to reinstate my certificate and boom – I was once again, a flight instructor.

When you do your 50 hours and get your first private pilot's license you're pretty restricted. You are only allowed to fly in clear blue skies, which means you can't fly under any circumstances with even the threat of inclement weather. You need to get your Instrument Rating to fly in bad weather. It's a difficult rating, and you have to pass a rigorous test with the FAA. Once I had my flight instructor's certificate back, I was able to train people to get that rating applied to their license. I had 6 students, 3 times a week at night. Meanwhile, during the day, I ran my business.

Matt introduced me to Brandon Rimes, a radio talk show host. I flew him and gave him flight lessons at Tampa North on the weekends. By meeting him, I was able to market my pest control business and talk about aviation on his radio show. People started hearing about me. I began networking more and both the pest control and my piloting took off.

The owner of Tampa North Airport in Lutz, Florida had a Barron I would rent to fly private individuals. I had the privilege of meeting high-profile people such as Tampa Buccaneers legend, Warrick Dunn. I even got the opportunity to fly Super Bowl Champion Coach and all around great guy, Tony Dungy. I had seen Tony on television many times, including on Monday Night Football and there he was, stepping onto a plane I was flying. It was a little surreal. Tony was actually referred to me by another law firm.

I got the call through networking with Brandon. " Hi Will, I'm the athletic director for a junior college in Mississippi. You were referred to us. We have a VIP we need flown here."

"What type of aircraft are you looking to utilize?" I asked. He chose the Barron, the least expensive plane we flew. "You sure you want to put Tony Dungy in a Barron?" I questioned. Again, Tony Dungy is a big deal to many people and me.

Jeremy from Blue Moon Transportation picked him up from his house to the airport. Flying commercial for the entirety of my career up till that point, I had never met anyone famous. I must admit, I was a little star struck. After that I started meeting more and more interesting, wealthy, and important people, including a co-owner of the Atlanta Falcons and one of my favorites, Ian Beckles, a former Bucs player and radio personality.

Due to the constant exposure from the radio show and networking, opportunities kept opening up for me. I created a LinkedIn account and a Facebook account. What used to work, hanging flyers on doors, etc., is no longer the way to get seen. Now it's best to get in front of groups and share information and get a Rolodex of people who can help you.

Many people don't understand the value of networking and being personable. They find it a waste of time and as a result, it's always up to that person to get his or her own leads. When you know how to network and make friends who trust that you can deliver, now you have every one of them looking to give you referrals from their circle(s) of influence. I went from a one-person sales team to a twenty-person sales team and I didn't even have to pay them. The people I networked with happily gave me referrals. In turn, whenever I could, I would send referrals their way. It was a win-win!

Take advantage of those opportunities to get yourself out there. You could have the best hot dog stand in Tampa but if no one knows you, you won't sell any hot dogs. You have to get exposure. That's one of the biggest parts of my success, networking and meeting people, being likeable and sharing with them my experiences in aviation.

Meanwhile, back at the pest control business, I found some great niches that led to a tremendous amount of work. I hooked up with people in the real estate business and networked with them. They always need pest control, termite inspections and repairs on the homes they are trying to sell.

I found the best way to drive business was by giving back to the community. I ran some eight or nine golf tournaments for charity. Recipients of the funds generated were groups such as the Shriners, St. Joseph's Women's Cancer Treatment Center and Hospice. I ran the tournaments at the Tampa Bay Golf and Country Club. We donated to local hospices who served first responders. Those folks would use golf carts to get to the houses quicker and they always needed funding.

This work brought two great things, a great sense of joy to give back and as a residual, clients. Lots and lots of clients. I ran a simple offer. If a customer signed up for thousand dollar pest control repair service, I gave 50% back to the foundation of their choice. Hospice, St. Joseph's, the Battered Women and Children facility would get half of their investment. People loved that they were getting top quality, all organic pest control while also giving back to their community. They got what they needed and also felt good at the same time. It was another win-win.

We only used organic chemicals, a derivative from the Chrysanthemum plant, the oil the plant produces is a natural deterrent for pests. Citrus also deters termites. These are natural ways to target pests. It meant we would have to come out to treat and respray more often but it was worth it. The longer the residual on a chemical, the more toxic it is.

Did I mention that I started all of this during the recession? People told me I was crazy to start a business at that time and that I was bound to fail. My answer to them: Oh yeah? Watch this! The truth is that money is cyclical, even during recessions, people make millions. I trusted that I could outwork the competition both in sales and in doing the job. I went 100 percent all in.

The pest control business and my work in aviation took flight, pretty much all at once. It got to the point that I could no longer divide my time between both without hurting one of them. I had to make a decision but there really was no choice. It was time to sell the pest control company. I had six different competitors who all wanted to buy me out and all six of them bid on the company. I felt that only one of them cared about customers the way we did and used the same products we used, so I sold it to him.

It was a long process and it was imperative for me to ensure that the work ethic of my company remained. Once I was convinced, I sold it to him even though he was not the highest offer I had, but he was the right choice. When faced with big moral decisions, it's about integrity. Money isn't everything.

One of the other people I met through the flying club was George Prasinos. He helped me get my license current again and I acclimated myself back to flying. The flying club managed several planes and they needed pilots. One of the planes was a Cessna 421 they managed for a local corporate law firm. They flew firm members and VIPs once or twice a month to various meetings.

I also helped the owner of Trans World Aviation build his General Operations Manual for a charter company. It's not easy to write but I was later able to repurpose it down the road and used it when I started my own charter company, Blumoon.

Another charter company out of St. Augustine, Florida reached out to us. They had a lot of calls for flights to and from Tampa Bay and needed help. I got the calls to fly government folks, representatives, lobbyists, lawyers and their clients back and forth from Tampa to Tallahassee. Many of them lived in Tampa but worked at the state capitol. So many interesting people were now clients. Politicians and athletes and all kinds of VIPs.

I became Captain Will Smith/ Blue Moon Aviation and worked hand in hand with my friend's company, Blue Moon Transportation. He would transport VIPs in luxury vehicles on the ground and I would transport them in the air.

I never thought I would fly again and yet, here I was! I had hit rock bottom and then sunk even lower. I had been incarcerated for something I hadn't committed. I had lifelong friends and family members turn their backs on me. I moved to a new state a broken man but still with goals and a fighting spirit. I started my life over again digging ditches and sleeping on a friend's sofa. But that was never who I was, those were the situations I was in. Don't ever let a situation define you. Who I was, always, was a person who believed in himself and who was willing to do what it took to live his dream life. Years later, I was back in the open skies.

My first time back in the air in 2010 was so invigorating! I felt as if the world's problems had simply lifted off my shoulders. I couldn't believe I was flying again! I was nervous but back on the bike and it was amazing. To be flying through the clouds into the clear blue sky looking down at Tampa Bay, I hadn't experienced that in a long time and I never thought I would again.

Excuses

- People can have a great idea but never follow through with it. They don't create an action plan. My nephew, a very talented guy, wants to own his own business. To say you're good at something and you have an idea that you want to work for yourself doesn't mean you actually will. An idea is soul-less. Actions and managing one's priority list is what takes an idea and manifests it into something tangible.

- Trying to find a good job is a full-time job. Once you find one, you need to spend 8 hours a day at least at that job. Whether you have just gotten out of prison, out of the military, or whatever, you will have to work during the day, even though it may be at something you don't want to do. Trust me on this, the day isn't over when you get out of work. Take night classes to learn the skills to do what you dream to do.

- Digging ditches got me to flying a jet. If I had never dug the ditches and met the people I met, I don't know where I'd be right now. 60% of life is just showing up. It's like going to the gym. If you can just get there, you've won half the battle. The word *try*, if you use it, means you've set yourself up for failure. People *try* to stop drinking, cussing, smoking, doing drugs. When you use the words I'm GOING TO that is what actually creates the type of momentum that results into action.

- I can imagine a big beautiful house with a swimming pool, but if I don't have the architectural plans for the house, how am I going to build it? My imagination has no arms or legs. It can't speak for me. Progress and goal-hitting take action and commitment.

- Also, always have a plan B. Plan A doesn't always work out. Never put all your eggs in one basket. A diversified portfolio is what wealthy people have. In life, if I don't have any sales this week, my weekend job is going to make me money.

- I have a back-up plan because I took the time and effort to accrue other skills besides flying. If, for whatever reason, I get grounded and can't fly, I can always go back to carpentry, sales, whatever – until the bad times pass.

- If I lose my company, I can always go back to flight instruction. People are always looking for good pilots and as long as there are insects and rodents, people will always need pest control. I worked on acquiring multiple skills. I know how to make that business run and succeed. I have options. I have skills. I have drive and ambition, which when exercised, gives me all I need to continue being successful.

- People work at one job for twenty-five years. When the Enrons of the world can go belly up and their stocks plummet. Take United Airlines after 9/11, people thought they had a pension but United took their money and put it back into the company. The stock price went to two dollars a share and many lost their retirement as well as their jobs. This is why you don't put all your eggs in one basket.

- You also have to create balance in your life. I'm not suggesting that you work fourteen hours a day, seven days a week. You need to have time management. Yes, I purposefully didn't date for a period of time but it was part of the plan for that to be temporary and it was. Personal time, family time, and vacation are all important. You have to be able to remove yourself from your work environment and think about yourself and your loved ones at least some of the time.

- Put stock in yourself. You're well being is part of the equation. Go fishing or golfing and take time to clear your head with whatever gives you peace of mind. It's mentally healthy. For years, I didn't have that luxury very often. I worked my ass off for five years but little by little I found my balance.

- You have to start someplace and that's the biggest piece, you have to START. Not think about starting, not planning to try to do something, you actually have to do something. Before you know it, you will be on the path you want and you will have time to enjoy the little things in life. You've got one life, just one. The world is full of abundance, make a plan for your future, work your tail off for it, and you'll achieve it.

Chapter 5

Make Your Bygones Be Bygones

You know the old expression, "Let bygones be bygones." It's one of those things that we paraphrase. Another expressions is, "If you keep one foot in tomorrow and one in yesterday, you end up pissing on today."

When my dad died, my sister couldn't understand it. She couldn't accept or process what had happened. "Daddy's gone, what am I going to do?" "Sis, Dad's dead, I know it's tough, but we need to move forward," was my answer.
I wasn't trying to be a hard-ass or unfeeling. I missed my dad too. Hell, I was in prison when he died and had no opportunity to mourn his death the way I would have liked. But I accepted it as a part of life and didn't let it derail me.

They say the 5 stages of grief are denial, anger, bargaining, depression, and acceptance. Here are three of the stages that I would like to focus on:

Denial: *Dad can't be dead. I'm having a bad dream.* We pretend as if it never happened and hope that he will walk through the door at any moment. This, of course, leads to constant disappointment.

Anger: *God! Why did you take my dad away? It's not fair!* We get mad at God, the universe, life, or the world. Oftentimes, we even get mad at the person who passed away. *Dad, why did you leave me? How could you do this to me?* This type of anger needs to be released as quickly as possible. I've seen people turn away from their core religious beliefs or have a hard time forgiving others and even themselves for many years after.

Depression: *I miss my father so much, I can't even function.* This way of thinking is crippling and can become an excuse for never being happy or living your life to the fullest.

I heard Dr. Phil once say that after twelve months, those who are still grieving the loss of a loved one, should seek therapy. Of course, it's hard to lose someone you love. But dwelling on the loss will do you no good. It certainly does nothing for the deceased. They are gone, you are still here. No one who ever loved you and left this earth before you would want you to spend the rest of your life in mourning. That's not love. That's ownership. Don't let the dead own you. They probably wouldn't want to even if they could.

There are three major pitfalls that keep us from succeeding from living an extraordinary life:

1. Excuses
2. Lack of confidence in oneself
3. Hanging onto the past.

You won't be able to deal with the things life throws at you if you are being controlled or others are enabling you. You won't deal with your own issues if you are constantly worrying about everyone else's issues. I have a friend who is a writer and her number one manifesto is, "Save yourself and the world will follow." It's not selfishness, it's common sense. If you're a mess, you can't help anyone else. Have you ever noticed that the people who are always complaining about how they have to clean up everybody else's backyard have a boatload of trash in their own?

If you become one of those people who are always focused on everyone else's problems, always helping your pals work through their issues, realize here and now that those people will suck the life out of you. Moreover, they will become your EXCUSE! You will use having to solve everyone else's issues as an excuse for not having time to deal with your own issues.

I'm not a cold-hearted guy. When people die, we should all go through a grieving process. Just don't make it an excuse for not living the life you should live. That won't do anything for you, and it'll dig you into a deeper hole. Understanding life is accepting it on life's terms, not your own, or you'll circle the drain and go down the pipes.

I have lost a lot of loved ones. I don't celebrate when they die. I know many do. They post on Facebook and other social media about lost loved ones, and it's obvious that they can't let go. One of the main reasons people never move forward is they're celebrating a death instead of a life!

The loss of a loved one tops the list of celebrating negativity. Many people celebrate the loss of a pet and post pictures of the poor animal on his way to be put down. Why not celebrate a remembrance of them versus a sad picture of their final days? Celebrate your memories, cherish them. This is positive and it not only honors them but enriches your life.

Let's take 9/11 as an example. Our entire country went into mourning. I know, because I was there in the thick of things. The morning it happened, I was at the airport assigned to check out a plane, routine for me normally. Two FBI agents approached me and started asking weird questions. In short order, I learned that the very plane I was inspecting was the one two of the terrorists had come in on that very day! Our country was brutally attacked in more ways than one. The aftermath of the attack resulted in people being distrustful of flying, so much so that the travel industry nearly came to a screeching halt. Not surprisingly, I and many other airline employees, were laid off.

But, despite all the pain and hurt we felt as a nation, I saw something great come out of it too. Instead of holding onto grief, I realized we could celebrate what we gained; how the country came together. There was no black or white, north or south, gay or straight, rich or poor. All of the things we argued about fell to the wayside. For a while, we were just Americans and we were united.

We're not ever going to celebrate the planes flying into the towers; we don't want to remember the horror. But, we can celebrate how we gathered together as people of all walks of life in one great nation.

When I went to prison, I lost more than time, I lost out on being present during important life moments. It was a special kind of hell knowing I was innocent and losing precious time away from my family, my sons not having their dad, my mom and sister not having me there when they needed me most, especially when my dad died. But, I don't dwell on that time in my life and stew in anger or regret. I don't even bother thinking about the people who put me in there.

The system was corrupt, and that sucked, but rather than wallow in self-pity, I did something about it. I brought the person who treated me unjustly to justice and helped other people who were also railroaded into jail by doing so. The judge who oversaw my case and used intimidation tactics on me was removed from the bench and lots of people were released from prison because I acted instead of folding. I later wrote a book about my experience. I helped inform people about the flaws in the system. I created awareness by making people see how the system can move against you, and how at the end of the day, prison is driven by funding and political achievements.

I went through something that could have broken me but instead, from the injustice and anger, I did something epic that I am proud of … and then I let it go!

I swam away from shore and got caught in a rip current. Life's rip currents can bring us far from where we once were, where we wind up when we finally get back to shore. We shouldn't blame the rip current. It was our own stupidity for not knowing we shouldn't have swum so far from shore. When we start to swim sideways and stop fighting it, we get past the riptide and can swim to shore but now we're at another beach. The good news is, you're on a beach! You can work your way back to where you were.

It's all about mindset. Sometimes we just need to listen to others who can give us guidance. Maybe you've accepted that you're lost – but I want to remind you, you're on a beach. You might not be where you thought you'd be in your life but you didn't drown. Instead you got taken by a current and now you're trying to get back to where you started from or maybe you just need to pick a new direction to go in from this new starting point. No matter what, it's time to get moving.

When you hang onto your past, you fight the current and when you fight the current, you'll be in it longer and possibly drown, never finding another beach.

Losing a job, ending a relationship, being backstabbed by a partner, being a circumstance of a bad environment, regardless of what has gone wrong in your life, you need to know there's an easy comeback. You simply close that door — you don't dwell on it, think on it, or complain about it — you just open another one.

Most people get upset at the action of something or someone but don't bother to think about the reasoning behind it.

- Lost a job? You were probably smarter than the owner and had more influence on the employees than he or she did. Maybe you should start your own business.
- Backstabbed by someone you trusted? The person was probably jealous of you. You had outgrown him or her. You are now free to get a higher caliber of friends who will help you instead of hate on you.
- Forced to file for bankruptcy? You're not alone. More than 80% of Americans are in debt. They don't own their houses or cars, the banks do.

Personally, I own my house, car and Sea-Doo boat. I practice what I preach and made a decision to buy only that which I could pay for up front. It took me a while to get there but the journey was well worth it.

I'm not saying don't build credit, just the opposite. In order to get credit, you need to have a history of debt. You need a minimum of a five-hundred credit score for a credit card and to get money to create success. What I am saying is, just don't live in debt, there's a difference.

I teach people to apply for credit cards for small amounts. Then, buy things and pay the amount off quickly. Rinse and repeat. Don't get so in over your head in debt that it takes you years to pay off or put you into a bankruptcy situation. It takes discipline to be careful with credit and

It takes discipline to be careful
with credit and debt, but it pays off.

debt, but it pays off when the time comes to buy something significant like a new car or a house. True fact, life is easier with a great credit rating.

Tomorrow is not promised, so make the most out of today. Set obtainable, short-range goals. Release the chains that restrict you and move toward the goal line rather than run toward the sidelines.

The law of attraction

You attract what you put out there. If you manifest fear, you will signal to the universe that you're not ready for good things to happen to you. If you manifest abundance, things will come pouring into your life to bring that abundance to you.

- Happiness begets happiness.
- Misery does indeed love company and will come and find you.
- Confidence will conquer fear every time.

Use vs. abuse

Never abuse leverage, use it. It's the difference between the bankrupt and the successful. In other words, never take more than you need. For example, I was eating at a fancy buffet one evening and I watched a guy walk up to the most expensive item on the table, the king crab legs. He loaded up his plate, nearly emptying the tray they were in and leaving very little for anyone else. I couldn't help but watch him, fascinated by this move. He was sitting alone, so all that food was intended for him and him alone. He started in on the crab legs but was full in short order. He only ate about twenty percent of the food on his plate, then left. The server came to clear his table, sighed, and threw the rest in the garbage. This man abused his leverage. Yes, it was an all-you-can-eat buffet, but the optimum word here is —*eat* — not all the food you can carry to your table. He had the leverage of having paid for the buffet but abused it by being incredibly wasteful.

When I was a kid, my folks wanted me to learn about the value of money and to understand finances. They gave me a cigar box and filled it with old checks and deposit slips, on which they had blacked out the banking numbers. Whenever I got money, I made out a deposit slip and put the money in the cigar box. When I wanted to buy something and use some of the money, I would have to fill out a check and leave it in there to show that I had withdrawn that money. It taught me how to use money and not abuse it at a very early age. The act of writing out the check made me think about what I was buying, and whether or not I really wanted or needed that item. I learned to use money, not abuse it.

Let's say you have paid off your mortgage on your home or enough of it to get a home equity loan. If you want to make significant improvement to your home, like adding a bathroom or building an addition that would add to the home's value, but instead you borrow that money and spend it frivolously, you haven't used that leverage, you've abused it! You'll soon find yourself in deeper debt but also with a much higher mortgage payment.

Embrace humility

There is no sense in coveting that which isn't yours. That fancy car your neighbor drives, that great girl your brother is dating, that job you didn't get – they're not yours, so don't be jealous of them. Look at where you are, what you do have that you can be grateful for, and humble yourself. Say, "This is where I came from and this is where I am now."

I spent twenty-six months in a prison cell. Was it the proudest time of my life? No, but it was part of my life experience and taught me a lot about being humble and being grateful for the smallest things.

That time I lost is never coming back. Once you lose something, it is never coming back. Stop waiting for it to return. If you lost time, learn to use your time wisely. If you lost a lover, take a little break. Get to know yourself a little better and be ready for a time when you may meet someone new so you can be the best possible version of yourself. You'll most likely find a better fit and that person will find a better you, which will make for a better relationship.

You cannot succeed unless you fail. People who have never failed will never understand what success is. Donald Trump failed many times, and now he's the most powerful man on the planet as the President of the United States. He had to fail over and over again to succeed. Most of our presidents have gone through that. You either win or you learn, there is no losing. Failure is not a loss; it's a learning experience.

Elon Musk lived in his car at one point in his life. Then he rose to fame and fortune. Now he's struggling again, hit with lawsuits and having to step down from his own company. But how long before he is right back on top again? Bets anyone?

If I had never gone to prison, I would not be writing this book. God knows where I would have been. I would not have learned all that I did from my 26 months in prison. It was the foundation of my success. Everything in life happens for a reason. I wouldn't have met Matt Fonk and had the chance to become a pilot again. By digging ditches to owning a pest control company, I made a path that opened doors for me. I'm grateful for the losses I experienced in my life; they put me on the path that led to my success today.

Be passionate about your work

People who have college degrees but are working dead-end jobs still have a degree. That degree still opens doors. If you're not using it to open a door for you because you want to stay in a box, it's your fault. If you're not working in your passion – every morning when you wake up and put your feet on the floor, if you're not excited about it, you might be in the wrong career.

Right now, people are happy with the economy, unemployment is the lowest since Reagan. I strongly believe that when people assert themselves and work and apply for the jobs they really want, they'll get them, especially when there are more jobs to go around than people to fill them. It's a great time to take advantage of this and go after your dream job or at least one closer to it or one that can lead you there.

I'm not going to apply for a civil engineering position if I want to be a pilot. Don't study law if you want to be a doctor. Hopefully, college graduates have thought it out and knew what they wanted to be. If it was to be a business owner, they got their business degree. That's what excited them.

If you earned a degree in nursing and you're a cashier at Wal-Mart, something went wrong. To say there aren't any job opportunities is no longer an excuse. Invoke common sense.

Find one thing you're passionate about. Seek your passion and do it well. If flying planes is your passion, if being a cop, or an attorney and protecting people is your thing, do it and do it well. Don't try to do five different things; you usually won't do any of them well. Give one hundred percent to your passion.

I got to my passion and I'm doing it well. Now I want to help others get to where they want and need to go. That's part of my passion as well, part of my mission here on earth. That's why I'm glad you're reading this book.

Chapter 6

Success Is a State of Mind

I had a philosophy teacher in college who taught us that success is a state of mind. He said, "There are three categories of people, the three R's: the random, the routine, and the reflective." I never knew how spot-on he was. As I journeyed through my life, I realized I could put everyone I knew in one of these three categories. Naturally, no one falls one hundred percent into one category, but by defining a person's characteristics, these categories hold enough room for everyone.

Random

Random people usually bounce from job to job. They're not career oriented, heck, they're not even job oriented. They generally don't last more than six to twelve months at any position. They're into get-rich-quick schemes and can get taken in by hucksters promising easy ways to make them quicker, bigger bucks without putting in a lot of work. They have very little direction and oftentimes live their lives with little options. For example, they're the type of people who can't choose which car to buy or what color. They are forced to purchase whatever they can afford. They rarely set goals or anything they can work toward. Their vision of the future usually doesn't range longer than the next two weeks.

Random folks are people who never owned a house or a new car. If they do work at one job, they get caught up in a vicious cycle and never get out of it. The job is a dead end, with little chance of advancement even if they applied themselves to advance. When they retire, they don't have much saved up. They live off of Social Security and their best retirement plan is hoping one of their kids do better than they did and can take care of them.

Random people often find themselves in trouble. They are the most likely of the three categories that wind up in prison. Once in that system, it's really hard for them to get out. When they do get released, they tend to go back to what they know, dealing drugs, stealing, or whatever put them in there in the first place. Many random people who get out of prison usually find themselves back in it because they don't think beyond their randomness.

If you feel that I'm describing your major characteristics, please understand that I'm not putting you down. I want you to know that I understand you and I'd like to help you. You still have time to get out of the downward spiraling cycle you are in. Think on this for a moment, how are you going to be living when you're sixty or seventy years old?

I know a guy who makes a multiple six-figure income washing storefront windows. He started out with an old pickup truck, a bucket, a squeegee on a pole, and some rags. He didn't even have a ladder. He began on one block asking store owners if he could wash their storefront windows for $5. Well, most of them said yes. Then he went to the next block and then the next. But he didn't just wash their windows once. He set up a schedule, returned to the same businesses at the same time on the same day each week. Today he has employees, 4 trucks and he supervises the work. He's retiring this year and his sons are taking over the business and will grow it even bigger. He had a plan and stuck to it. What I'm trying to share with you is that no one has an excuse to not be successful.

What if no one is there to help you or Social Security finally does run out of funds? Even if you get it, how much have you paid in? Will that be anywhere near enough to put a roof over your head and food on the table? You might be the prettiest stripper on the block and having a blast right now but sooner or later no one is going to want you twirling around a pole. You have to prepare for retirement. Are you really all right with inconveniencing your children or family to take care of you when you're seventy or eighty?

You have to prepare for retirement.

Random doesn't just happen with people who are low income, uneducated, on drugs or not terribly smart. There are many people who have grown up in the lap of luxury, having every advantage in the world, who can also be categorized in the random section. Those are the ones who eventually, even Mommy and Daddy stop bailing out.

Look at most professional athletes. There are thousands of them who are not super famous. For the brief time they're playing their sport, they are getting paid extremely well compared to the average person. Not only are they paid well, many of their living and travel expenses are generally covered by whatever team they play for. For all of their successes on the field of play and in the real world, they don't think more than two weeks ahead or set any long-term goals. By the time they're tenure in the game is over, most of them have spent the majority of their money and have no game plan for the future.

They are then forced to swallow their pride and work regular or even menial jobs. At one point in their lives, thousands of people were cheering for them, less than ten years later they are greeting people with, "Welcome to McDonald's, how can I help you?"

Random people rarely even make it to middle class. They're rich on Friday and broke on Monday. Smile if you know people like that. Smile wider if that's you!

The Prison pit

About 77% of those who wind up in prison get out and go right back to it. They basically become institutionalized. They're creatures of habit. The sad thing is that once you get into the system, you're caught in a trap. People don't want to hire you. Doors are slammed in your face. I know, I've been there. The record shows your charges even when they're dismissed. I was initially charged with first-degree rape. It took me 8 months to get them to drop that to dismiss it. Three months later, I was reindicted on a 2nd degree. The judge tried to hang that charge on me just to look good and wanted to make it stick. It was frustrating, and even though I was innocent and eventually set free, it was hard to get a job.

In Florida, everyone does background and drug testing. If you've been in prison, very few people will give you a chance. It's not fair. If a person has done their time, paid their debt to society, they need support. Just recently, Floridians voted to allow people who have been charged with a felony and have returned to society, the right to vote in elections again. Fair is fair. Rights are rights.

A guy I grew up with went to jail at eighteen on a capital murder charge. He didn't kill anyone but he was an accessory and therefore was guilty by association. He did twenty-six years in prison. During that time he was totally rehabilitated. He came out all those years later with a completely different way of thinking. He's not the cocky kid he once was. He deserves a chance to start over and is making the best of it.

The sad reality is that the entire system is broken. Prison is big business today. If we fix people while in jail, help them to become good citizens so they can get off of the hamster wheel, the prison industry will fail. When I left prison, I didn't receive any counseling. No one sat me down and said, "Will, before you get out, let's talk about your future. I want to make sure you never wind up here again."

When you get out of prison you have some big questions to answer. Who are you going to live with? What are you going to do for work, transportation, food, or clothing? There are halfway houses and while that can be helpful the same mentality that brought people to prison runs wild in there. As a result, many struggle to find a job. At least now there are lots of jobs available but many come with very low pay and few benefits, if they'll even consider an ex-con.

So, what do you do? My answer was and is, if you can't find a job, make a job. Mow lawns, shovel snow, wash windows, do whatever you can to make money and be your own person. Every person in the world has skills. If you're healthy or relatively strong, you have skills. If you're not healthy but can read and write, you have skills. What skills can you use?

Society also needs to have a heart. We need to help these folks become successful. More people in prison are mentally ill than you can imagine; the stats are astounding. We're not doing anything for them health wise, so they wind up in prison. So many people were on depression pills in the eighties. Women were taking Prozac like it was candy. How much of that affected the next generation? Is it possible that lots of people are the chemically imbalanced products of that?

The problems are many and the solutions are unclear, but to help people move out of the random category, we need to recognize that it's in all of our best interests to make that happen. Productive people are useful to a society, not a drag on it.

Routine

Most people fall into the category of routine. These folks are generally classified as the middle class. They graduate high school, most go to college, get a degree, work for a company and stay in the workforce for 40 years or so, then retire. They don't want to become entrepreneurs. They're happy making their $60 - $90K. They brush their teeth at 8, eat breakfast at 8:30 while they read the paper, and are at work by 9. They leave work at five or six and follow a similar routine with their home life. They live their lives content and secure, going through the same routine over and over again.

And you know what? There's not a damn thing wrong with that, but they don't really strive to be better. These are our bankers, accountants, salespeople, and store managers. They pick a profession and do it for the rest of their lives. They don't like to get out of their pattern. If their routine is having a drink after work, they do it all the time. They tend to vacation at the same place once a year, buy gas at the same gas station, eat at the same restaurants, and live in the same house for most of their adult lives.

The majority of people are good with that. The truth is, we need people who do the day-to-day work. They fill a lot of jobs that someone needs to do. What would you do if there were no bankers, insurance salespeople, barbers, or even teachers for that matter? We need them. They are not a drag on the rest of us. In fact, as I stated, that's most of us! They pay their bills on time and make life easier for most of the world. They take care of themselves and their families and generally don't look for a handout.

Reflective

But then there are ... the reflective people. They have a different kind of mindset. They are driven by an insatiable hunger, a fire in their bellies to do more, to become more. If they make a million, they shoot to make three million. If they make a hundred million, they shoot to make three hundred million. They never look at success eye-to-eye. They keep their goals constantly out of reach so that they're always pushed to do more.

Biggie Smalls once said, "More money, more problems." The reflective people will easily take on more problems if it means more money.

He may have been right, but the reflective bunch have a different kind of mindset, a hunger, a fire in their bellies to be bigger. They want to make hundreds of millions a year or more. They never settle. Make no mistake about it, the reflective people, although some can be wildly successful, aren't always liked. The thing is, once you get there, it depends on how you handle all of it. The smart ones are humble and don't forget where they came from. The not-so-smart ones think their money and fame takes the place of manner and common courtesy.

Nicolas Copernicus – the Renaissance era mathematician and astronomer who formulated a model of the universe and was the first to place the Sun rather than the Earth at the center – would caution that the higher you go, the further you have to fall. It's always important to know that if you get too close to the sun, you're going to get burned and it's a long way down.

Trump, Turner, Gates, and Musk are not random or routine people. They are reflective thinkers. Reflective thinking and the concept of how to handle wealth can be associated with Socrates. These are two of his most famous quotes and are the basis for much of his teachings and methods.

1. "Wealth does not bring goodness, but goodness brings wealth and every other blessing, both to the individual and to the state."
2. "Life without examination is not worth living."

How does that play into today's reflective thinkers? Toyota is a great example. They do everything they can to try to break their cars to improve them. Talk about examining your life. In contrast, Ford doesn't do that; they're happy with the cars as they come off the line. Toyota is reflective and Ford is routine.

Always question why something failed so as to make things better. Reflective people say, "I had a good day today, but how can I make it better tomorrow? What steps did I accomplish, what else could I have done to get to my goal of becoming a millionaire, to be the best at something, to make the world a better place?"

Ultra successful people are focused on how to make something better. The appliance company, LG, is a very interesting company. They don't make products, they make products better. In other words, LG's job is upgrading other people's work. They're not reinventing the wheel; they're making it better. Guys like Trump examine things and ask, "Why did this deal fall apart? How can we win next time?"

Reflective people get bored with good. They are constantly striving to get better. They're in competition with themselves more than with others. Olympic swimmers want to beat their personal best. It's not just about beating a world record. It's about beating the best time they ever achieved.

I think that everyone should decompress and reflect on their day, each and every day. Take the time to look at how to improve your situation. If you've had a bad day at work and yelled at someone, reflect, maybe apologize the next day because that person may not have deserved it. If you've had a good day, how can you build on an experience that made it good?

Never forget Karma - what goes around, comes around. It's foolish to do negative things and expect positive results. If we surround ourselves with reflective people, we become that, the same with random and routine people.

I love the old saying that if you lay down with dogs you get up with fleas. There's a popular Spanish saying that goes: *Dime con quién andas y te diré quién eres*, which translates to, tell me who you walk with and I'll tell you who you are. It's so true. You become a product of your environment. Hang out with people who will elevate you and take you to the places you want to go. Join a writing group, take a class, volunteer at a non-profit whose cause you believe in. Help others. It will help you more.

Good is the enemy of great

It's a mindset. Some people let their situation control their own outcome instead of controlling their situation. The deck was stacked against me, I was wrongfully accused, I lost years of my life in prison and even when I was released I had a criminal record that followed me for a few years. I could have accepted my fate. I could have said, *'Well, at least I'm not in jail!'* and accepted that I'd never get ahead in life again. But I don't have that type of mindset. I didn't become a pilot in the first place by thinking like that and although the world tried to derail me, it hadn't changed who I was. In my mind, I didn't have a choice but to be successful again. I was okay digging ditches because it was all I could do and it was going to put money in my pocket while I figured out the rest of my life. I'm not of the random category, I reflected, planned, and acted. I didn't accept my fate, I reinvented it.

In my mind, I didn't have a choice but to be successful again.

What you do becomes your norm. People get comfortable with where they get to and are scared to go after something better. I spent two years at a pest control company and stepped outside the box. I got reflective. I was working with pesticides that can cause cancer, so I started a company that used products that would eliminate the pests but were healthy for the environment. That business opened up the doors for me to start flying again.

Each time I left one job to go to another, it was elevating me closer to my goal. A random person, making $8 an hour in one place would leave for another $8 job somewhere else. They never go forward, they just move laterally. They will always be an employee, always sweating and grinding to make someone else's dream come true. I did do a bunch of different jobs, yes, but they weren't lateral moves, each move was a step up.

Allowing yourself to be random might even mean you just bounce around in the same industry. I had an employee who worked for every pest control company in the area. He never made more money with any one of them than the other, even with all his experience, because he never built tenure with any one company. And he never took the chance to strike out on his own. He had all the knowledge in the world to start his own business but he never did. It's as if he never knew that without risk there's no reward in life. In order to succeed, you must fail.

If you see yourself as random, you can skip over the routine part and go straight to reflective. Many people's goal is not to become reflective, it's to have tenure and security. There's nothing wrong with that as long as you have a goal that's far enough to stretch you yet still be obtainable.

Look within yourself

Where do you want to put the mark? Some people's mark is to stay twenty or thirty years working for someone. They're not entrepreneurial. They join the military, work at a software company, become police officers, teachers or nurses. Thank God for them, and I personally thank them for their service. I have a good friend who retired from the military then went on to join the Tampa Police Department. He retired from the force and is now flying planes with two retirement incomes. That's the way to do it!

Some people are like gypsies, nomads, or wanderers. To each his own as long as you have some way to take care of yourself. Lots of young people today are discouraged. They are drifting, wandering. We need to show them that they can have a future. We need to ask them, "What do you want to do when you get out of high school or college? What would excite you to take on as a career?" Young people today care less about money and more about people, about the world and about enjoying life. They invest in causes more than in stocks and bonds.

Being altruistic can be helpful. The news is negative and all about ratings. They don't care who they hurt. TV is not helping. Burying yourself in gaming is not a lifestyle. Most people don't become highly paid gaming experts. Most kids who can toss a football don't become NFL players by watching the games on TV.

People need to set some realistic goals and those of us who can, need to offer guidance. It's not fair for the reflective to pay for the random. Depression, mental instability, drug use is rampant. Why are some parts of the homeless population huge in certain places and not in others? What are the issues and how can we solve that crisis?

As we grow up, our environment changes us from little bundles of joy to the people we become. Some people just seem to be born with internal moral fortitude. It's hard to say how or why. Something you've done or something that happened along the way, got you where you are. Don't let that situation define you. Make it fuel you!

It's easier for a twenty-five-year old to start over than sixty-five-year year old, we only live so long. If you're sixty-five and your goal is to bring in $100K into retirement, it would have been much easier if you had started at twenty-five. If you're getting out of prison, in recovery from drug addiction, stuck in a dead-end job because you didn't finish your education, the first thing you need to do is create income; lick stamps, dig ditches, do whatever it takes.

My thought process is, if I can't start a job, I'll create a job. Many parolees complain that no one will hire them. That's an excuse. Make a job if you can't find one. Mow grass, pull weeds, deliver groceries, help people move – find a need and fill it. Clean cars – you can start with very little money – a bucket, a towel, and cleaning products. Start a pressure washing company. Minimal start-up costs, and your sweat equity will pay off.

Education is also a key. There are still a lot of Pell grants available. If you're a single mom, someone just out of prison, these are grants you don't have to pay back. So later, when you apply for a small business loan with a degree, you look good. Banks won't lend money to people who haven't proven to be able to manage themselves financially. Leverage yourself. Show you're worth the loan.

Education is everywhere. There are tons of free courses online. Coursera and Udemy offer a huge array of courses on all kinds of topics. You can learn just about anything that interests you. The library is open to anyone and learning there is free. Instructions on how to do anything from cooking to changing the oil on your car can be found on YouTube, all for free. Mechanics fix your car and charge you $85 an hour. Are you handy with tools? Look up what to do to fix the car yourself on YouTube. Learn to do things for yourself. You'll save money and grow as a person. Plus, you will add to your skillset and make yourself more valuable in the workforce.

Wouldn't you like the type of life where you're excited every morning to go to work? You might have to eat a little crow, so suck it up buttercup, it's well worth it. Once you get yourself going, keep going. It might take hard work, going to school at night or working two or even three jobs, but again, it's worth it. Remember, I'm not saying anything hypothetically, this is exactly what I did.

I was able to get an apartment pretty quickly. I lived there for a year and then bought a house. Four years after getting out of prison, I got off my friend's couch, had my own vehicle, and had my own house. I whistled every morning going to work, not because I loved the job so much, but because I loved the path I was on. Like I said, it's all about mindset.

If you find yourself in the random category, I'd love to help you break the cycle. Together, we can do anything.

Chapter 7

Breaking the Cycle

The definition of insanity is often said to be doing the same thing over and over again and expecting a different result. We humans are creatures of habit. We simply default back to what we know in most cases, even if what we know isn't yielding positive results. So, if we are trying to drastically change our lives, how do we do it?

Here are my three steps to effecting major life changes and moving from the insanity of repetition:

1. **Wipe the slate clean**

Whatever bad habits you've gotten into, be it drugs, or alcohol abuse, jail time or any bad behaviors and habits that took you down the wrong path – let it all go. Stop beating yourself up about your mistakes. Appreciate the fact that every day is a new day and you are given a blank slate to fill up that day however you wish. Get up early, take a hot shower, put on fresh, clean clothes and act like it's the first day of school and you're excited to learn.

2. Let go of the past

I know this may sound like I'm making things trivial that may not feel that way, but to move forward, you have to stop looking backwards. Put all the hurt and pain and mistakes you've made in your rear view mirror and don't look back. That crap will kill you. Besides, what will it change? It's done. You can't change the past. You can't fix it and looking at it is just rubbing salt in a wound. Let the good things that happened in your past live peacefully in your mind and help build your confidence in your future.

3. Use the Benjamin Franklin decision-making process

Basically, Franklin's process for making difficult decisions was a matter of listing the pros and cons, taking time to reflect on them, and then making the best possible decision.

Here are the steps he used to make important decisions:

• Frame the decision you need to make

Ask yourself a simple question that will require a yes or no answer like – "Should I look for a new job?"

• List the pros and cons

Draw a line down the center of a piece of paper. Write down as many pros on the left side and cons on the right as you can think of. Take your time with this. You may move some pros to the cons and vice versa and more may come to you.

- **Consider the importance of each of the pros and the cons**

Rate them from 1 to 10. Very important would rate a 10, barely important would rate a 1. Use the number scale for each one based on your opinion of their importance.

- **How likely is it that these pros and cons might happen**

If a pro or a con is certain to happen, rate it a 10. Very unlikely, rate it a 1. Give anything in between your best guess and a numerical rating.

- **Give the pros and cons a numerical weight**

Multiply the rating for Importance times the rating for Probability. A pro that is extremely important (10) and is likely to happen (5) gets a weight of 50. A con of extremely high importance (10) but not really likely (2) gets a weight of 20. Make sense?

- **Review everything and spend time thinking about your final decision**

Look at all the factors and make the best decision you can.

Be as resourceful when finding ways to improve your future as you have been for finding a drug dealer or a bad relationship. You can use the Ben Franklin method in a different way. Get a piece of paper, draw the line down the middle, and this time put all the things on one side that would keep you in the same loop of insanity and on the other side the things you want to manifest in your life.

The insanity side might have things like, keep doing drugs, hanging out with the same crowd that got me in trouble, or staying in a bad relationship. The other side might be, take a class, get a better job, make new friends or reconnect with old ones who don't get into trouble.

On the left side list of things from your past, such as the bad stuff that took you down the wrong path. On the right side, list the things that will keep you from going back to the stuff on the left, things that will help you accomplish new and better goals.

Sometimes we have to change people, places, and things. I know that sounds daunting but it's not as hard as you think.

Sometimes it's as simple as changing your environment. It may seem impossible to move to a new city or a new state but it may be the best thing you can do. Moving away from the people who somehow influenced you or even encouraged you to drink, do drugs, commit crimes, will be a game changer. The trick is to not seek the same kind of people in a new place. Take moving as a chance to reinvent yourself. Hang out in different kinds of places.

If you hang out in bars, you will likely meet people who drink and even do drugs. If you join a gym, you'll meet people who are health-conscious. The more you go, you might even get a discount or free classes. If you go to a church, you're more likely to meet people who are trying to better themselves from the inside.

Hang out with people you want to be like. Volunteer at a non-profit that helps other people. Join a softball or bowling league, join a meditation group or a book club at the library. Be true to yourself and delve into your passions and interests.
The main thing is to KEEP BUSY! The old adage is true; an idle mind is the devil's workshop.

Create a workout plan. One of my favorite expressions is, *Wealth is Health.* I'll get into that a little more in depth later in this book. But I'll share this with you now; you can't buy health. It has to be earned. There are no shortcuts. Healthy body, healthy mind, healthy spirit. It all goes together. Working out will give you endorphins. It's a better and different kind of high, one that will enhance your life, not put it in a state of limbo.

One thing to be aware of is that you can't withdraw from people all together. We all need interaction with other people, just not negative people. You have to change your habits. If you start drinking, you're likely to go back to your old habits. If you attend AA meetings regularly, you will meet other people who are trying to break bad habits or people who have done so and are trying to pay that forward by sponsoring others.

Do a fair bit of self-reflecting. How did I get here? Where do I want to be? If you haven't heard of the term vision board, let me enlighten you. It can be a big piece of cardboard or even the mirror above your dresser. Attach pictures of who you want to be or where you want to go in life. If you want to be a lawyer, tack up pictures of a person in a suit, carrying a briefcase and walking into a law firm or sitting behind a big shiny desk. If you want to be a soldier, paste pictures of people in uniform up there. If you want to live in a log cabin by a lake, tack that picture up. Visualize the things you want, the person you want to be. The power of visualization is a real thing, utilize it.

You need to have a goal and then connect the dots. Determine a realistic timeframe. It may take 1 year or 2 years or more but have that in mind. Maybe you'll decide to be a server in a restaurant full-time while saving enough money to take classes in college at night for

Determine a realistic timeframe.

the next 2 years. Maybe by year 3 you work only part-time as a server while building a side business until you get your degree and go into business full-time.

Have a plan. It may change, you may have to rethink it or regroup, but without a plan, you have no roadmap to follow and you'll drift. It takes courage to rebuild ourselves – our own temple – it could be many years to rebuild but you need a plan just like an architect needs blueprints.

If you've gone through a bankruptcy, you need to learn about budgeting and balancing your expenses against your income.

If you're dealing with alcoholism, you need to face it. Stop making excuses and kidding yourself. Self-awareness is tough for most people. "I'm a social drinker, not an alcoholic. I function at my job, in my relationships. I just like to drink just about every night." Really? Guess what? You're probably an alcoholic. You need to take steps to stop drinking. Stop hanging out in bars or with people who drink for starters. Consider AA meetings. At least go to a few and meet other people who have been where you are and probably a lot worse. It's good to get an understanding that it can get worse so you can turn that ship around before it sails. And yes, you're going to need to learn self-discipline to get where you need to be.

Finding your serenity will help with every aspect of changing. Wouldn't you love to be excited about each day of your life? Don't you want to welcome the sound of your alarm clock because you're excited for another day? You can get there! But to do that, you have to learn to love yourself first. I know, big cliché but guess what? Clichés are around for a reason. They are largely true.

You have to create a strong relationship with yourself. You can't depend on others or them on you. You don't need an enabler and you don't want to become one. Ironically, lots of people who cling to their enablers become enablers to others. It's a viscious cycle. Stay out of it.

Did you know that most heart attacks happen between the hours of 7 and 9 am? That's because that's the time most people are headed to the jobs they hate going to. They don't have inner peace. They haven't found their serenity. They focus on work and all the things they have to do that they don't want to do instead of loving themselves enough to do the things that make them happy.

You can find another job. You can educate yourself and learn a new skill that excites you so that you wake up happy and excited about the day ahead, each and every day. That's a by-product of loving yourself too.

I am a big believer in reflective thinking, looking at the positive aspects of the day and pulling the good out of even a bad day. There is always at least one thing that was good. If nothing else, you survived it, you're still here, still breathing and tomorrow brings all new possibilities. Maybe it's just that you had a good sandwich for lunch. There is some good in every bad thing. Find it, reflect on it at the end of each day, and move forward toward tomorrow.

Remove the word "try" from your vocabulary. When you say you'll "try" to do something, you're saying you probably won't. Don't try, do.

There are many different ways to break the cycle. Everyone's situation is different and you have to connect with the issues you have that may not be someone else's issues. It's very personal but it can be done.

It's especially hard if you've been in prison and are stepping back into the outside world. People are in prison for a variety of reasons. Many people think that prison is the end of their lives, even if they're in there for five or ten years. The truth is that society is rooting for you! That's why there are skills or trades you can learn while in prison. Even in prison you can begin to equip yourself to be better.

Unlearn the habits of hurting others, of getting over on others, of only thinking of yourself, and apply your time cultivating the better side of you. If you want people to trust you, learn to be trustworthy. Give out what you want to get back. Sure, there are always bad people out there but you don't have to be one, and from now on, you don't have to hang out with them.

It's hard to break the cycle if you have a long-standing family history of problems like alcoholism, drug abuse, sexual or physical abuse, but it can be done. Some of the most successful people in the world have come from some of the worst situations. They've come from poverty, dealt with racial prejudice, have had only one parent or worse, foster parents who only cared about the check and not about them. You need to know that you have it within you to break whatever generational curse is plaguing you.

We've talked a lot about identifying the problems, facing them and changing. In the next chapter, we're going to talk about how. Action speaks much louder than words, and we are going to get into real action plans that will get you on the path to break whatever cycle you've been spinning in. Let's go!

Chapter 8

Health is Wealth

Are you living a great life if you're making great money but have poor health? Can you fully enjoy your life if you're constantly sick, fatigued, achy, going to the hospital, and loaded up on meds?

The rat race we all seem to be racing is to get wealthy. It seems that everyone's goal is to live debt-free, to go to whatever restaurant we want, to get a new car every year, to buy a home and a summer home, and to be able to afford pretty much what our heart's desire. That's not a bad goal. In fact, the premise of this book is to help you live a better life in many areas, including becoming wealthy.

However, you're missing the mark if you think this book is all about financial gain. It's not. It's about wealth. Wealth in your finances, sure, but also wealth in your state of mind, wealth with your circle of

Wealth in your finances, sure, but also wealth in your state of mind, wealth with your circle of friends, and wealth with your health.

friends, and wealth with your health. This book is about improving your life as a whole. I would be remiss if I didn't write a chapter about catering to your health. After all, health, when broken down to the least common denominator, is wealth.

There's a balance to all things. When things get off balance, there is confusion, panic, and disorder. The best way to start balancing your life is to start from within.

I don't know who you are, you may be a runner, an athlete, or you might be slightly overweight or even obese. Regardless of how you are physically, everything I put in this chapter will apply to you. If you're not healthy physically, maybe you drink a lot, smoke too often, do drugs, just lie around the house eating sweets, you're creating an imbalance in your life.

When there's an imbalance, people usually try to overcompensate. For example, if we're very tired at 3 p.m., we might drink another coffee. If we feel that we get too tired too often, we resort to drinking energy drinks all day. What they don't know is that what they're doing to feel better actually makes them feel worse in the long run. For example, energy drinks might give a pep to your step when you take it, but the sugar and other things in those drinks are the root causes of many deadly illnesses.

Ironically, although science and the study of human beings continue to grow, the worse we are becoming! The government and big business – including Big Pharma that regulates the foods we eat and the medications we take –

– don't seem to be working on our best interests. They're not working on feeding the people intelligently, they're working on feeding their pockets and their stocks. If you want to get healthy, you're on your own. The government or your doctors aren't going to help you much.

When I was growing up in the late '80s, therapists all over the country were giving women tons of anti-depressants. That's what Big Pharma said they needed. A generation later, we have children being diagnosed with Attention Deficit Hyperactive Disorder (ADHD) at an alarming rate. It's really an epidemic. It would seem that just about everyone suffers from some form of ADHD, including our grandmothers who are on Facebook, Twitter, and Instagram! The therapists in the '80s, just like the therapists now, are incentivized to keep many people medicated. Unfortunately, medical doctors are stuck in the same predicament. They're forced to offer certain medications in order for the insurance companies to pay them. It's almost something from a Sci-Fi movie, except it's true.

I'd like to help you find a way to circumvent the system with some practical ways to get or stay healthy. The first thing I'd like to impress on you is that everything starts in the gut. Great health and diseases all come from the gut!

Let's start with your morning routine. When we sleep, we slowly dehydrate. You may not feel dehydrated when you wake up but that doesn't mean that your body doesn't need water. Most of us go right for the java. Some people's first intake is the smoke from a cigarette. For some, it's an energy drink. The first thing our bodies need in the morning is water, H_2O! Drink two glasses of water before you put anything else in your system.

Water is of major importance to all living things. You may have learned this in school — our bodies are made up of 60% water. Your body is almost never craving water. When we drink water, it doesn't just hydrate our bodies, it also hydrates our brain. I'm not saying to forego your coffee, I'm suggesting that before you drink your coffee, first drink some water. For the record, however, I am saying to forego your cigarettes and energy drinks, they're no good for you. Shoveling coffee and donuts into your system every morning is not the breakfast of champions, it's the breakfast of the asthmatic.

While I'm discussing what to do in the morning, I need to mention the poison many loving parents are feeding their kids. Most cereals are the worst things possible to eat. Read the article written by Mary Kekatos, a health reporter for Dailymail.com, published on October 24, 2018, entitled, *'Cancer-causing' weed killer is found in Honey Nut Cheerios, Quaker Oats, and twenty-four more cereals.* Click or type in this link to see the entire article at https://dailym.ai/2RSTHFA.

I'm not a certified health guru but I know common sense, and common sense tells me to do my homework before I eat or give my children any type of cereal. The artificial sugar in most of them is horrible for our bodies. There are also untold amounts of pesticides in cereals.

There are other foods from very lucrative companies or restaurants that you should also avoid. McDonald's French fries are right near the top of the list. They put enough pesticides in their potatoes to kill a horse! In fact, McD's potatoes absorb so many chemicals, they need to let the potatoes sit in water for months in order for them to be safe for human consumption. To know more, click on this link to see the findings by author, journalist, activist, and professor of journalism at the U.C. Berkeley Graduate School of Journalism – Michael Pollan https://theheartysoul.com/mcdonalds-fries-pesticides/amp/

Even things we eat that we assume to be healthy can be dangerous to our bodies. We live in a world where chemicals have become a necessary part of our farming practices. An article by the www.thestreet.com published on January 18, 2018, written by The Street Staff, lists these three popular fruits and vegetables with the most pesticide residue: strawberries, spinach, nectarines. To read the rest of the article, follow this link: https://bit.ly/2Rdwi9r.

My point in this chapter is this: to live a better life, it would help if you had better health. It's hard to go after your new goals relentlessly if you're grossly overweight and/or hopped up on medications. If you hang around overweight people struggling with eating right, you're most likely going to struggle to eat right. It's the same thing with your mental state, if you hang around with jerks, you're going to be a jerk. If you hang around with winners, you're going to be a winner. Enthusiasm breeds enthusiasm, it's contagious.

We are a nation of overmedicated people. There's a pill for everything. But like I said, everything starts in the gut. If you start to eat better, starting now, in a few months, you'll probably be off many of the medications you might be on now. You're mental state will be running at an optimum level. You're energy level will be naturally high so you won't need sugar-filled pick-me-ups. Your attention span will allow you to focus more on the task in front of you so you can reach the goal ahead.

Health is where wealth starts and ends. If you're not wealthy financially, start with getting wealthy physically. There is no way that a version of you who is healthier and more energetic will produce the same results that you are producing now.

Health is where wealth starts and ends.

The time is now. It's easy. Start with a glass of water.

Chapter 9

Common Sense Is Not So Common

Have you ever watched the news and you were shocked at a story and thought, *what in the world was he thinking?* There are just some things that people shouldn't do. It's so obvious that people shouldn't do them that nobody tells them not to do it. However, time and time again, I hear a story about someone who got hurt or went to jail for doing something so stupid, I'm left wondering, *does that person have any common sense at all? Or, maybe they ate one too many McDonald's cheeseburgers!*

If you look at the news and some videos on YouTube, you'll agree with me on this, common sense is not so common. Whether it's some knucklehead on a motorcycle trying to jump off of a flimsy ramp (only to drive straight through the ramp and crash with whatever object is in front of the ramp), or jogging at midnight wearing black clothes and no reflector (only to be hit by a car) or trying to rob a liquor store through the ceiling (only to crash through the ceiling, land on a rack of bottles of wine, to then fall with the wine to the hard linoleum floor with bottles of wine smashing all around them, to later finding out that the door doesn't open from the inside and now he's trapped till the cops come). I'm not making up hypothetical scenarios, I've seen videos of all these things happening!

I commend you, wherever you are in life. You might have everything going on in your life the way you want to or you might be in serious debt, in prison, unemployed, or dependent on medication to get through the day. Regardless of where you are in life at this very moment, I commend you for wanting to better yourself.

Motivational speaker and sales guru, Zig Ziglar used to tell the people who came to hear him speak that they were the best and the brightest. Not because of where they were in life, but because they invested money and time to learn how to better themselves. "Eventually," Zig would say, "you are going to be the business leaders of the present." And he was right, many people who once heard him speak made millions of dollars and went on to have incredibly lucrative careers.

Unfortunately, not everyone who goes to those events actually applies what they have been taught. That just doesn't make sense to me. If you're going to go hear from someone who is ultra-successful, and you take an entire day or two to see him and you pay hundreds or thousands of dollars, why aren't you going to apply what he says? While I commend you for wanting to better yourself and for reading this book, I want you to commit to actually applying what you learn within these pages. Not to do so just isn't smart thinking.

Think for yourself

Too many people are like bobble-heads glued on the dashboard of a car. They'll say yes or no depending on what the popular opinion is the same way a bobble-head shakes yes or no depending on what turn the car

They'll say yes or no depending on what the popular opinion is...

makes. Marketing companies today are literally geniuses. They know exactly what to say, how to say it, and how to display their products. News companies are also geniuses, they know what buttons to push to upset you about the other party and they play to your fears. They don't care if what they say is 100% correct. As long as you're watching, they'll be happy.

They just care that their ratings go up, which means commercials get charged more money during their show, which means everyone from the owners to the janitor can take home more money. Sadly, this leads to people being easily manipulated by news that at times isn't entirely true or is one-sided. Even sadder, millions and millions of people watch these shows and because they don't know how to think for themselves or even question the validity of these news shows, those half-truths become people's opinions! Regardless of which news outlet you watch, CNN, FOX or MSNBC, listen to what they're saying but also think for yourself.

One of the biggest trends today, as I write this, is the vape craze. Young people from all over the country are vaping, thinking that it's harmless because there's no tobacco involved. Guess what? Sitting in a car full of vapor just can't be a healthy situation for you! Would you rather breathe fresh air or manmade vapor? It seems like common sense to me but this vaping thing really is sweeping the nation.

Have you ever met those people who are so proud that they blurt out whatever they feel like? They pound themselves on the chest with pride, "I tell it like it is!" No, moron, you're acting like a five-year-old. Why don't you try engaging your mind before you actually engage your mouth? There are adult attributes called restraint, patience, and kindness. Take your mom's advice and don't say anything if you don't have anything nice to say. Common sense!

If you're working toward a financial goal, let's say you're saving up to buy a house, don't purchase a $30,000 car! People who work on fixing their credit will inevitably get a letter from a credit card company or two informing them that they've been approved for a an $18K or $30K loan for a car. What do these people do? Mind you, they're saving for a house. They buy a car! Sure, you get the car but then you'll never get the house. Common sense!

If you're a high school graduate and going to college. I know you might be thinking that it's time for you to party and sow your wild oats but think ahead. Don't get saddled up with hundreds of thousands of dollar's worth of debt. I know many students who work full-time while going to school so that when they graduate, they can start making money for themselves and not a financial institution. Why pay back money for twenty years of your life for a four-year education? Some people with Ph.D.'s live broke because the loan they have is at six or eight percent, so the first eight to ten years they're only paying back the interest on the loan. The good news is there are all sorts of grants at your disposal. Look into a Pell Grant or something that matches up with your background. Wouldn't you rather have someone else pay for your college? Common sense!

Don't get emotionally involved with someone until you are emotionally happy with yourself. Common sense!

Don't start a family if you're unable to support yourself. It costs a minimum of $250,000 to raise a child from infant to graduating high school. If you're having trouble finding steady lodging and food, it's not the time to have kids. Common sense!

On that note, if you have children who you can't support and you need the government to help you out, don't have any more kids! I'm not knocking government assistance; I take pride because I live in a country that helps out its citizens when they are down and out. Sure, there are many who abuse the system, but on the whole, they are necessary. There are many kids who grew up eating the government cheese that broke the mold of their family and made something out of themselves. My point is that if you have five kids, and the older ones are out of control, even though you have government assistance, and you have a tough time putting diapers on your babies, don't have more kids. Common sense!

Being on the phone, texting while driving ... is that text worth your life? When I drive on Davis Island – near a college campus – I have to pay special attention to the road. Not because of traffic, but because many of those drivers are watching their phones as much as they're watching the road. There was one time when I would have been hit head on had I not slammed on my horn. The pretty young blonde student looked up from her phone just in time to swerve and not hit me head on. When you drive, put your phone down. Common sense!

If you want to get a raise, but you have frequent tardiness. You undermine your boss at meetings because you're so much smarter than him and you want to prove it. You brag to other people how much of a better job you would do as the boss. Do you really think you're going to get a raise or promoted with these sort of actions on your part? If you want a raise or a promotion, befriend your boss because he's the only one who can get you the raise or promotion. Common sense!

If you don't have another job, try not to cuss out your current boss, biting your tongue to keep your job is worth having food on the table for you and your family. Keep your job while you look for another job. Once you get an interview for another job, don't cuss out your boss. You haven't gotten the other job yet and you might need him for a reference. Common sense!

Don't be the type of person who's rich on Friday but broke on Monday. You don't need to buy every drink for your friends. It's not your duty to feed the freeloaders who always have their hands out and mouths open. Live within your means. Don't go out to restaurants every day. Go to the grocery store and stretch your money. Find new recipes online and make yourself better food for half the price of restaurants. When I got off of my friend's couch and into my own apartment, I would make sausage bread that I would eat from for four days. The sausage, cheese, cilantro, and rolled up bread only cost me eight dollars. While most of the people I worked with would go out to eat for lunch, I would eat my packed lunch from home. It was healthier and cheaper. Common sense!

It's not your duty to feed the freeloaders...

Find time for serenity and peace in your life. My serenity is my boat. I own a waterfront home, right in front of a large lake. When I need to detox from my busy flying schedule, I trade my pilot-captain hat for my boat-captain hat and relax. At night, I'll make myself a drink and sit by the stone bonfire I have on my back yard. I make sure to spend time, not only training my mind, but also relaxing my mind. If you're constantly on the go, you're going to wear yourself out. Find ways to let the negativity and stress out of your life before a doctor prescribes you medication to do the same thing you can do yourself. Common sense!

You have one life to live. Go all in. Invest in yourself. Why live a difficult life when you have it in you to live a great life? Common sense!

Chapter 10

7-Step Awareness and Success Plan

I commend you for getting to this final chapter. Some of this may have been hard to take in but in your effort to better your life, you continued on reading. However, as you end this book, it is going to leave you at a fork in the road. Reading from a book and actually applying what you've learned into your daily life are two separate things. The big question is: What are you going to do with the advice given?

7–Step Awareness and Success Plan

1) Recognize your situation

If you're in a bad situation, are you going to continue to do the same things that got you there? How's your bank account? If it's not where you'd like it to be, are you going to do the same things that produced such little savings? Look around you, at where you live, at who your neighbors are, at how clean the place is, at how much space you have, and if you're not living where you'd like, surrounded by the type of neighbors you would prefer, are you going to do the same things that got you there?

Are you recently freed from being incarcerated? Do you have limitations due to legal matters? If so, accept what you did to get yourself there and start making a plan to get out of whatever situation you're in. Maybe due to being a poor student or dropping out of high school or not caring about your life very much, you may not qualify for an office job wearing a suit and tie. However, this is still the land of opportunity. There are many people who are living great lives, some are even millionaires, who started right where you are, with no job, no education, perhaps even a criminal record – and yet they made it. You can too. It begins with taking a good look at where you're at. If it pisses you off that you have let your life get to a point you hate, do something about it.

2) Stop making excuses

Life is tough. Life is unfair. I get it. I had everything I wanted in my life until I got sent to prison for something I didn't do. When I got out, I worked from sun up to sun down in the Florida heat, I get it. I had a legitimate gripe. I could have gone to court and gotten a judge to decide in my favor that yes, I got screwed over. But, what would that have done for me? Not a single thing!

One of the main reasons why people don't better their lives is because they're too busy making excuses for the lives they currently have. It's always someone or something else's fault. There are adults who blame their situation on the fact they didn't have a father. There are adults who blame their situation on the color of their skin. There are adults who blame their situation on the language they speak. There are people who blame where they grew up. If that's you, it's time to stop looking at the world solely through your lens. The truth is that there are plenty of successful people who didn't grow up with a father, that are of every race and color, and who live in the United States but barely speak English.

Your excuses only work to keep you where you are. They

Your excuses only work to keep you where you are.

don't work to put you to work, they don't work to make you money, and they don't work to get you out of whatever bad situation you might find yourself in. Stop playing the Blame Game; it's for losers.

3) Prioritize on what's important

Is partying more important to you than being able to get up early in the morning and getting to work on time? Is it more important than having your own apartment? The problem with many people who never get to live the life of their dreams is that they don't know how to prioritize their day.

There's a terminology in aviation called "Load Shedding." Basically that's what pilots call it when they have to transfer electrical power in the aircraft from one area to another. The problem with many people is that they spend too much 'electrical power' on things that won't benefit them. Look at what's important. Food, sleep, and health – those things are important. Yet, people focus more on booze, drugs, and sex. Sure, those things can be fun but let me share a little secret with you — it ALL gets better if you have more money!

If you prioritize your day right, you'll find that there's plenty of time to do what's important to you. There are twenty-four hours in every day. People have become millionaires using up the same twenty-four hours you have. You have enough time to live a great life; what you need to do is prioritize your priorities.

4) Surround yourself with the right people

Jennifer Cohen, a contributor to *Forbes Online*, wrote an article on December 4, 2018 entitled "Surrounding Yourself With The Right People Changes Everything." She starts the article by stating that it's widely known that one of the best ways to improve on a skill is to practice with someone who's better than you. For example, if you want to learn how to play tennis, play or practice with someone better than you. Sure, you'll have sore muscles but eventually, you'll get better. You might even get to the point where you're so good, you can help someone else get better.

Can you imagine trying to get better at tennis playing against someone who doesn't know how to play? Can you imagine trying to learn tennis from people who hate tennis? In the article, she calls those types of people, Negative Nellies.

I think it's time you took inventory on how many Negative Nellies you have in your life. Look, life is hard enough without having naysayers throwing negativity at you at every turn. If your friends get drunk every night, smoke weed or do drugs daily, do you really need them in your life? You might say to yourself, "Well, I do that too!" Again, I get it. But if you're ready to stop doing that every day and work on living a better life, it'll be easier for you to get a new circle of friends.

Some people have told me, "I can get rid of my bad friends, but it's my family members that are holding me back." My answer, "Then get rid of them too!"

It's YOUR life! Not your sisters, not your brothers, not your stepbrothers, not your cousins, it's your life! Regardless of what blood runs in someone's veins or if they share your last name, that does not give them the right to hold you back from making something great out of yourself. I'd rather be alone than be surrounded with bad company.

Find people who are more successful than you. Find people who are striving to do something great. The right people around you makes a huge difference as to the type of life you will live. If you hang out with criminals, you'll end up in jail. If you hang out with Christians, you'll end up in church. If you hang out with people who care about their fitness, you'll end in gyms.

If you hang out with people who care about their fitness, you'll end in gyms.

gyms. If you hang out with entrepreneurs, you'll end up starting a business. If you hang out with writers, you'll write a book or blogs. The better the company, the better your life will be.

5) Sacrifice

It feels as if some people view sacrifice as a bad or outdated word. They might refer to young YouTube personalities who get millions of views on their channels making good money and think, *see, it's easy to be successful.* The reality is, for every successful YouTube personality, there are a million others who struggle to get 50 views.

Leadership Guru John Maxwell, author of *New York Times* best-selling book, *The 21 Irrefutable Laws of Leadership*, said, "Everything of value is uphill." Meaning, whatever it is that's good, you're going to have to work for. He recently spoke at Grant Cardone's 10X Conference in Miami in February 2019. The speaker lineup was amazing, not only did he speak, but Daymond John of the hit TV show, *Shark Tank*, was also there as was the first self-made woman billionaire, Sara Blakely, the founder of Spanx and young multi-millionaire, Russell Brunson, the founder of Click Funnels. The event was so big it had to be held at Marlins Park, the home of the Miami Marlins.

The stadium was packed with more than 35,000 people who all want to better their lives. As John Maxwell was describing how everything of value is uphill, he said, "No one who ever became very successful, when asked, 'How did you do it?' looked around and said, 'Gee, I have no idea!' That's because success doesn't happen by luck. It requires a level of sacrifice.

If you're in college, sacrifice some of the parties to study. If you're in prison, sacrifice time in the yard and go to the library. If you're trying to lose weight, sacrifice the sweets and have some fruit. Those things will all pay off in the end. You have to stop being so shortsighted when it comes to rewards. Instant rewards, such as partying, are like fast food, it'll fill you up but too much of it will give you problems in the long run.

Sacrificing means being consistent. The more you do something, the easier it becomes to do. The more you stay in and study, the more you save money, the more you take online courses – the easier they are to do over and over again.

6) Find a goal

You need to have something to shoot for. If you get in a car and have no idea where to go, who knows where you'll end up? Find a goal that suits your personality. Some people might want to become a new anchor. The problem is, they don't read well, their faces are full of tattoos, and they don't like wearing suits. That's not the right goal for that person! Find something realistic that matches your strengths and your abilities.

A person without a goal is like a ship without a rudder. It'll stay afloat but it's pretty much useless.

If you've gone through step 3 and got rid of the bad karma around you and you've surrounded yourself with good people who are going to help you or cheer you on, figure out what do you want to do with your life. Do you want to be a nurse, a doctor, a teacher, a lawyer, or a business owner? You can't score a touchdown if there's no goal.

Start with your long-range goal. Think of how you want to live your life ten or fifteen years from now. What type of house do you want? What type of spouse? What type of career? Once you've verbalized it, go ahead and write it down. Once you've written it down, read it over and over again and start to visualize your future self living that type of life.

Next, figure out what it's going to take to get you from where you are to your dream life.

7) Work your plan

Now that you've identified the life you want to eventually live, it's time to create a plan to get there and then to work that plan. Your first step might be to get a job. So, get a job. Don't be picky; you don't have to be married to it. Start bringing in some income so that you can buy some better clothes to interview for a better job.

Let's say you want to become pilot but on the way there you will need to make money for tests and flight school. You're big and strong and heard that a local nursing home is hiring orderlies. Plan out how you're going to get that job so that you can then start flight training.

Maybe you're going to need to pay for an accreditation. Okay.

How much is that going to cost? $500? Okay.

When do you want to take it? In eight weeks? Okay.

How much do you need to save weekly to save up the $500? $62.50. Okay.

How can you save that money? By making coffee at home and giving up Starbucks coffee and by not going out every other Friday night? Okay.

Following that plan will get you the job as an orderly. Now, figure out the steps it will take to get you into flight school. Once you have that figured out, work that plan. Make sure to have short-term goals that align with your long-term goal. It's really that easy or that hard, depending on how you look at it, to becoming successful.

Once you have that figured out, work that plan.

Plan out your life in bite-sized, actionable steps. If you try to get to ultra successful from where you are in six months, you're going to set yourself up for failure. Move forward, slowly but steadily. There will be times when you move faster and other times when it feels like you're moving too slowly. The thing is to keep moving towards the goal.

I'm here to help

I didn't write this book because I have nothing better to do. I also didn't write it because I love to sit down and write. I'd rather be out flying or spending time with my loved ones than working on a book. But I can't stop and think of how down and out I once was. The only thing I had to my name was a criminal record. I had no money and no options. However, today I fly to the most beautiful places on earth.

My goal is to be philanthropic. Being a giver doesn't always have to do with giving money, although I do that to the charities that I support. Being philanthropic also means giving of your time, energy, and wisdom. That's why I wrote this book.

My goal is to help those who are downtrodden, broken hearted, defeated, railroaded by the system, and those who just don't know how to get out of the hole they are in. By every measure, I've become successful. I don't say that to boast, nor do I say that to belittle anyone. I say that because if I can do it, I think many others can too. The problem is, they don't know how. While I'm not a financial advisor, a licensed counselor, or someone with a Ph.D., I know what I did to get out of the hell I was living and made a great life for myself and I can teach others to do the same.

You can find more information about me at www.captainwillsmith.com. If you'd like me to speak to inmates, troubled teens, or any other group, I'd be delighted to do so. My contact information can be found in the About the Author section of this book and on my site.

To those of you in the struggle who have finished this book, I'm also making myself accessible to you. On my site, you'll find out how to get in touch with me. It would be an honor and a privilege to help you find and then live your dream life.

You only die once, but you get to live every day. Make your life the best it can be.

About the Author

Captain and two-time author, Will Smith currently lives with the love of his life Ericka, in the Sunshine State – Florida. He is the proud father of two boys, Will and Giff.

He was raised in a divorced environment, living with his mother and visiting his father. His mother, Lillian Smith, worked three jobs to put young Will through private school in his early and middle school years. Upon graduating public high school, he went on to play football for a Division 1 college.

Captain Will has been flying planes for more than 25 years. A former commercial airline pilot, Will is now an on-demand flight instructor and the President and Owner of Blumoon Aviation.

As much as Will loves to fly, his passion lies in helping others. Being a serial entrepreneur who has built businesses and sold them, he is a highly sought-after speaker. He does his best to make himself available to speak when asked. As a speaker, he's a common fixture at prisons, entrepreneurial events, and financial conferences.

When he's not flying or encouraging others, Will enjoys golfing, family time, and spending time on his boat with his family and friends.

For more information on Captain Will Smith, please visit:
www.captainwillsmith.com

Acknowledgments

I'd like to thank Ericka Ciancarelli for her love and support. You are my strength.

My mother, Lillian Smith, for never giving up on me, even when it felt the rest of the world did. You're my backbone, and I am who I am because of you.

Will and Giff – you may not know it but you are my inspiration. Knowing that I am your dad drives me to succeed and forces me never to expect anything less than the best from myself.

Larry Brindley – for always being there for me. I cherish our friendship more than you know.

Matt Fonk – Thanks for helping me get back amongst the clouds.

Eli Gonzalez – thanks for helping me put my words on paper. You have a true gift, my friend.

The Ghost Publishing – Lil Barcaski and the rest of the team, thanks for believing in me and for all your hard work getting this book out to help others.